BrainWords

How the Science of Reading Informs Teaching

BrainW🧠rds

How the Science of Reading Informs Teaching

J. Richard Gentry   Gene P. Ouellette

Stenhouse
PUBLISHERS

www.stenhouse.com

Portsmouth, New Hampshire

Library of Congress Cataloging-in-Publication Data:

Names: Gentry, Richard, 1949- author. | Ouellette, Gene, 1967– author.
Title: How the science of reading informs teaching / Richard Gentry and Gene Ouellette.
Description: Portsmouth, New Hampshire : Stenhouse Publishers, [2018] | Includes bibliographical references.
Identifiers: LCCN 2018037243 (print) | LCCN 2018043460 (ebook) | ISBN 9781625312747 (ebook) | ISBN 9781625312730 (pbk. : alk. paper)
Subjects: LCSH: Reading (Elementary) | Reading–Physiological aspects. | Reading, Psychology of. | Reading disability.
Classification: LCC LB1573 (ebook) | LCC LB1573 .G397 2018 (print) | DDC 372.4–dc23
LC record available at https://lccn.loc.gov/2018037243

Cover design, interior design, and typesetting by Page2, LLC, Wayne, NJ.

Printed in the United States of America

This book is printed on paper certified by third-party standards for sustainably managed forestry.

25 24 23 22 21   4371   9 8 7 6 5 4

This book is dedicated to those who help bridge the gap between the science of reading and best classroom practices and to all who have devoted their energies to helping children succeed on the pathway to literacy.

Contents

Foreword

It's an exciting time for those of us who teach reading.

Not only is science continually uncovering fascinating information about how human beings read, but researchers are showing us how we can use this evolving knowledge to more effectively teach children to read, write, and spell. And that's what this book by Dr. Richard Gentry and Dr. Gene Ouellette is all about: the science behind reading, the new types of instructional practices that spring from that science, and the urgent call that we can help a lot of kids if we get moving on it.

Even though reading is the most widely studied area of theory and instruction, our understanding of how reading works in the brain continues to expand and deepen. At this very moment, somewhere in the world, a researcher is illuminating an area of reading development that was only dimly lit just a year ago, or even a month ago. Cleverly crafted experiments are associating types of instruction with gains in reading ability. Eye-movement cameras are connecting physical systems to theoretical understanding. Functional magnetic resonance imaging (fMRI) machines are enabling neuroscientists to link brain biology and reading behavior.

We've recently learned that when a person undergoing an fMRI concentrates on a pattern within a word, one section of his brain lights up more than the others. But, the result is different when the person considers a whole word. What's more, the brain area that is activated during pattern noticing (i.e., decoding at a sublexical level) influences the area activated during word noticing (i.e., word reading at the lexical level). This finding is important. It tells us something about how the brain works, and it points toward more effective ways of teaching word reading.

Research headlines about discoveries like this appear regularly. *Word learning selectively sharpens orthographic representations. Invented spelling helps young children develop phonological awareness. The visual word form area in the brain is critical to reading success.* In time, these headlines lead to instructional practices that produce larger and longer-lasting gains in reading, writing, and spelling skills. These gains, in turn, enable more children to reach critical reading and writing benchmarks. This is especially thrilling news.

Richard Gentry and Gene Ouellette are not only caught up on this news and the excitement—they're generating it! Cannonballing into the reading research pool, they're making waves, and these waves are moving the field of reading forward. In this book, Richard and Gene explain why it's imperative that children develop "a deep level of knowledge of words in the brain" and tell us exactly how we can help our students gain this deep level of knowledge. Spoiler alert: It's not done through solitary phonological awareness activities, isolated decoding lessons, or separated vocabulary, fluency, and comprehension instruction. Rather, it is accomplished through instruction that is holistic, integrative, and complementary.

In this discussion, the authors highlight how orthographic learning is critically important, invented spelling is the starting point for explicit teaching of word reading skills, and spell-to-read instruction aligns with the brain's reading circuitry. These are essential points. But the heart of Richard and Gene's book is the idea of *brain words*.

A brain fully stocked with brain words is necessary for fluent reading. Both children and adults need encoded words—thousands of glorious, splendiferous, enchanting words—to make their reading engines run. And as you read this book, you'll want to immediately start helping your students store letters, patterns, and whole words in their brain dictionaries. What are the best ways to do this? Gene and Richard begin by encouraging you to rethink reading instruction. This challenge isn't an attempt to catch the latest bandwagon or a reaction to the most recent pendulum swing. It's not frivolous. No, it's rooted in thirty or more years of research, as well as today's neuroscientific findings.

With this in mind, the authors give new ways to look at content and instruction. Thankfully, Gene and Richard have done a great deal of reading, understanding, and summarizing for us. They take research findings and present them in an easy to understand way, and then they translate these findings into actions we can take in our classrooms.

For example, they correct misunderstandings about what, exactly, "sight words" are, and they offer more effective methods for teaching them. For teachers of kindergarten and first-grade children, they share practical examples of reading and writing development, provide a clear view of word reading instruction, and give a template for creating integrated lessons that support brain word research. These lessons include phonological awareness, phonics, decoding, encoding, and sight words. And for second- through sixth-grade teachers, they give specific ways to continue building the dictionary in the reading brain.

Isn't it amazing how spelling, sound, and meaning work together to allow human beings to read? At some point, speech sounds are associated with squiggles. We learn these squiggles are letters that represent sounds. When we put letters together in a specific way, we create a word that has meaning. In time, this word can be read by sight. Next, words are strung together to convey a thought, idea, or feeling. Then, before you know it, the world is bursting with sentences, paragraphs, and pages that communicate beauty, anger, joy, despair, adventure, deception, truth, and love. Wow. If that isn't exciting, I don't know what is.

So, get ready to learn what brain words are, how they are used during reading, and how you can flood student brain dictionaries with them. I'm convinced that when you read this book, you'll get caught up in the excitement. But here's the thing: reading doesn't just happen. Someone has to teach kids how to do it. This is why teachers are some of the most important people on the planet. This is why your service is very much needed in our world. And this is why I hope you'll take the exciting explanations and instructional revelations presented in *Brain Words* to the level of action. Immediate action.

It's important that we apply the knowledge that Richard, Gene, and many other hardworking researchers have gained through their sustained efforts. The message that "brain words are critical for successful reading and writing" is one that should be heard by educators around the world. When we bring reading instruction into alignment with science, foundational skills expand and deepen as our students grow to become happy and successful readers, writers, and spellers.

That's a result that all true teachers live for.

— Mark Weakland

Acknowledgments

I would like to express my gratitude to the school administrators and teachers alike who through their commitment to uniting science and teaching have welcomed me and my research team into their schools and classrooms over the years. I am also appreciative of my family and the patience and support they exhibited through the writing of this book; special acknowledgment is given to my wife, Katrina, not only for her support but also for her contributions to the book as a teacher of over twenty-five years.

With gratitude,

Gene

My career as an educator spans over forty years. I have been blessed to have worked with numerous teachers, educators, and scholars including giants in the fields of education and psychology who have helped shape my thinking. I acknowledge my mother, Bonnie Wright Gentry, who taught me to read as my first-grade teacher and inspired my career. Special gratitude goes to families and children who have shared their children's writing and personal accounts of literacy development including the Meigses, the Jensens, the Gillets, the Pindzolas, and the Seredicks. A special thank-you to my friends Susan Sturock and Bill McIntrye and heartfelt appreciation to Bill Boswell for twenty-five years of support.

With gratitude,

Richard

CHAPTER 1

Rethinking Reading Instruction as Building a Dictionary in the Brain

For the past two decades, flatlined reading scores have plagued schools across North America, and the message is clear: too many of our children are not learning to read well. Shockingly, 65 percent of American school children read below grade-level proficiency according to the National Assessment of Educational Progress (NAEP 2017). The international media as well as scientists in cognitive psychology and neuroscience have not been silent about this unacceptable state of affairs surrounding reading education, arguing that the cause lies in the gap between what we know about the science of reading and how reading is actually being taught in the classroom. The past two decades of scientific research have brought forth an explosion of new knowledge about the architecture of the reading brain and the development of the neurological reading circuitry, but teachers, administrators, and even our academic teacher-training institutions remain largely unenlightened by this work. So the state of reading education in North America is far from optimal, and this compels us to ask ourselves the question—why? Are we afraid to listen to science? Why do we keep on trying what doesn't work? How can the science of reading guide us in teaching students how to read?

This book is designed to help fill in the gap between the science of reading and what we do in the classroom by explaining reading theory, research, and the neurological reading circuitry in ways that teachers can understand and clearly relate to their classroom instruction. These new understandings will help you recognize some of the mistakes made over the last two or three decades and guide you in how to fix them. Although much of what is done in reading instruction may be well intentioned, there is a crucial missing link that metaphorically we refer to as "building the dictionary in each child's brain."

When we speak of building a dictionary in each child's brain, we are referring to building a bank of syllables and words within each child—that includes information on pronunciation, meaning, and, critically, spelling. These stored patterns and words, referred to by scientists as *lexical representations*, we refer to here as *brain words*. As we will explain throughout this book, brain words are key to developing rapid and accurate word reading. And word reading is a necessary skill to master on the pathway to literacy.

We have too much confusion about teaching word reading. For some teachers, a word study program may consist only of word sorting and hypothesis testing so that kids can "discover" how words work. Others may follow complex "comprehensive scope and sequence" charts, which are said to bring systematic exploration of words into the classroom but too often lead to isolated lessons pulled from a kit. Instead of support in understanding how the reading brain works, you get a book full of bulleted items and little guidance in how to make sense of it all. In most classes we see separate, disconnected lessons for phonological awareness, phonics, vocabulary, and the like, and you are expected to stuff them all into your already overpacked language arts block. This leaves you befuddled trying to figure out how much time to spend on each component, how to sequence them, and what to prioritize or leave out.

Perhaps you do word study lessons required in your district but feel pushed to move on due to too many disconnected components or lessons to cover—whether all of your students get it or not. You might feel equally confused by lessons based on words that are randomly pulled from whatever story, persuasive piece, or informational text comes next in your reading program, and you can't see how it all connects. Or maybe your school's approach to word reading instruction includes optional, add-on minilessons or activities that seem disconnected, or even worse, perhaps word reading isn't even specified in your school's curriculum. And then there's spelling. How does spelling fit into literacy instruction? With all these issues, chances are that explicit spelling lessons aren't being taught at all in many schools today. State and even national accountability assessments rarely include a direct measure of spelling competence, and you may wonder what students at your grade level should have mastered because the spelling you see in their writing can be just plain scary.

But it doesn't need to be this way. Brain research and educational and cognitive psychology tell us a new story about what word study and reading instruction should look like and what its outcome should be—better reading. In this book, we rethink how students can best be taught to read based on current science and knowledge of the reading brain.

The Missing Piece: What the Science of Reading and Research Tells Us About Building a Dictionary in the Brain

Too often we teach reading and word study lessons without giving consideration to the science behind learning to read and the brain development that supports it. Teaching students to read isn't about lessons pulled from a kit or reading program or pulled together in a piecemeal fashion; instead it's about fostering developmental changes within each student's brain that lead to improved reading. The missing piece of effective reading instruction enables the brain to become specialized for reading so that it can store brain-based spelling representations. This process is called *orthographic learning*, and the resulting brain-based representations are what we call *brain words*.

Although spelling has received short shrift from influential policy-making documents such as the report from the National Reading Panel, Common Core State Standards, or similar national and state standards, we will show you that spelling is crucial for building brain words and successful reading. If your literacy teaching and word study lessons don't take word learning to a deep level in your students' brains so they can create brain words, it may not be the best it can be.

In this book we'll help you rethink reading instruction and word study as a more effective way to build these dictionaries in the brain where students can store and automatically access sounds, spellings, and meanings for correctly spelled words—connecting to other essential reading circuitry in the brain for meaning and understanding and resulting in more proficient reading and writing. These dictionaries are built slowly in the early phases of breaking the complex code of English. As students gain knowledge of the alphabet and important phonological awareness, they become able to

KEYPOINT

Have you ever traveled to a new country and learned to pronounce the name of a new city or a food that you tasted for the first time? When you returned home the name of that city or food was in your language system; you could hear it, say it, write it, and read it correctly and with understanding. If so, you added a brain word.

decode or sound out simple words. Over time, students start to create brain-based spelling representations, their brain words, to make reading and writing more fluent and efficient. As you will see in subsequent chapters, word reading pathways, brain words, and the reading brain itself all continue to be built, refined, integrated, and used throughout one's literate lifetime. The more you read and study and experience life, the more words you add to that dictionary in your brain.

When we reconsider reading instruction and word study through the enhanced lens of the scientific study of reading, we can greatly improve current educational outcomes by increasing the number of students who read well, think well, and write well. By implementing an approach to teaching word reading that is based on developmental theory, research, and brain study, we can add the missing link to what has been left out of literacy teaching, standards, and expectations.

A Spell-to-Read Approach to Teaching Reading

In this book, we recommend a spell-to-read approach for teaching reading, based on developmental reading theory, research, and brain study. In this science-based approach, we flip the typical sequence for teaching on its head. Instead of exposing students to print and expecting them to magically become readers, we present words aurally first and then ask students to analyze the sounds they hear. We encourage students to then spell the word how they hear it or how they see it in their mind's eye in self-directed attempts often referred to as *invented spelling*.

> **TERMINOLOGY TACKLED:**
> ## Invented Spelling
>
> Sometimes called creative spelling, child spelling, or sound spelling, *invented spelling* is the child's self-attempt to spell a word that the he or she can't spell correctly.

This process both activates and promotes phonological awareness and engages students in a deep, self-directed analytical process. Brain regions known to be critical for reading are also activated and become integrated in the process. The result is increased processing and engagement that starts students down the pathway to creating brain words. Importantly, as outlined in chapters to come, invented spelling is not the final outcome but rather the starting point for explicit teaching that targets word reading skills.

The prioritization of brain words and our spell-to-read methodology aligns with how the brain's reading circuitry works. Think of spell-to-read methodology this way: if you can spell it, you can read it. As you read across this page, if you have highly academic brain words (some from experience in specialized academic areas, others from life experience), perhaps you can spell words such as *nanoengineering, demurrer, gastroenterologist, eschatology, suffrage, sufferance,* and the like. If you can decode these words, you likely hear the word (in your mind), are able to say it (using your speech and language system), can read it, and attempt to write it. But if you can spell it correctly and match it with meaning, then you can both spell and read the word and likely know it and use it appropriately. Even more common words such as the homophones *karat, carat, carrot,* and *caret* that you see on this page and read easily may challenge you personally as a speller in matching each with its correct meaning. If you see *caret* out of context do you comprehend it? Taking each of the four words deeper in your brain by matching the sound of the word with its spelling and specific meaning makes it a brain word. As we will review in upcoming chapters, brain words are best established through the act of spelling. And brain words support more efficient reading. It's that simple.

Rethinking reading instruction and word study in this way is directly linked to building better functioning neural pathways for word reading and comprehension. New information from cognition psychology demonstrates how having a deep level of knowledge of words in the brain—including how to hear them, say them, read them, and spell them correctly—turns out to be a very big deal. Yet for too many reading programs, establishing a dictionary of brain words is either missing or attempted through teaching methods that aren't scientifically supported. Instruction is all too often piecemeal—failing to integrate this brain connection and neglecting the aural component of written language. For decades schools have given instruction in deep word knowledge—including explicit spelling instruction—very low priority while touting phonological awareness alone, phonics only for isolated decoding lessons, and vocabulary, fluency, and comprehension as separate entities without capitalizing on their essential deeper connection to word reading and spelling.

Adding Brain Words to Your Classroom

Of course rethinking reading instruction and word study will not replace all of what you are already doing. For example, the word reading skills targeted in this book presume your students are learning the alphabetic principle and can name many letters and give their associated sounds with fluency; we build upon that knowledge. Without the alphabetic principle as a foundational skill, progress in word reading becomes challenging to say the least.

TERMINOLOGY TACKLED:

The Alphabetic Principle

The *alphabetic principle* is the understanding that each grapheme or letter (or in some cases a group of letters) must map onto a sound or phoneme. Children who understand the alphabetic principle know that letters represent sounds that form spoken words.

We build on the work of excellent resources available for teaching alphabetic knowledge (e.g., Reutzel 2015). But we also show how the alphabetic principle is greatly enhanced in early phases by teacher scaffolding of invented spelling because development of alphabet knowledge is facilitated by the approximations that are part and parcel of invented spelling.

Rethinking reading instruction and increasing focus on word reading will also not replace contextual reading activities or other teaching that focuses on known important areas such as phonological awareness, phonics, vocabulary, fluency, and comprehension; these are all vital elements of reading instruction. Rather, the discussions in this book are intended to add to your teacher knowledge and, most importantly, give you effective research-based tools to add to your current instructional practices to make your teaching more efficient and effective—to the benefit of all students.

The Book Ahead

In the chapters ahead we'll start with an academic overview to show that what we have to offer is a fresh and new way to connect research, science, and classroom practices and then continue with five goals in mind that will help you understand the science behind effective reading instruction and word study in ways that can dramatically improve literacy outcomes in your classroom:

Goal 1 Rethink reading instruction and word study as a better, more efficacious way to build each student's dictionary in the brain (i.e., brain words), which leads to more successful readers and writers.

Goal 2 Provide a concise, readable, academic treatment of the current status of what science says about how children learn to read and how the reading brain works in support of science-based classroom practices.

Goal 3 Clear the fog surrounding current reading instruction with a new vision into best practices enhanced by a spell-to-read approach.

Goal 4 Present a clear view of word reading instruction for beginning readers tied to the science behind developmentally appropriate K–1 reading, writing, and spelling development.

Goal 5 Take you beyond grades K–1 to show how to continue building the dictionary in the reading brain in second through sixth grades, which is critical for continued progress throughout elementary school and into the middle grades.

TERMINOLOGY TACKLED:

Phonological Awareness and Phonics Are Not One and the Same

Phonological awareness refers to an understanding that words are made from syllables and sounds; it is the ability to hear and manipulate these units of sound. *Phonics*, on the other hand, is an instructional method that teaches letter-sound correspondences.

Understanding current developmental theory and research can help bridge a three-decades-old gap between reading research and practice. Here in plain language we'll map out the science and start to look at specific strategies and tools it suggests for your classroom. We will take on some provocative topics and maybe even step on your toes a bit when we very frankly discuss instructional practices that just don't work as well as we've been told. We'll give you examples of effective reading instruction and word study along with easy-to-use formative assessments that can fit with whatever reading program or methodology you are using.

CHAPTER 2
How the Scientific Study of Reading Can Inform Teaching

. . . presents an overview of the scientific study of reading. So many beginning reading teachers are frustrated with how to find time to work on phonological awareness, decoding, encoding, and teaching sight words, all as separate lessons, not to mention what to do about spelling. Chapter 2 brings you good news from the current field of science and will explore how developmental and cognitive research presents a clear scientific rationale for integrating all of these—phonological awareness, decoding, encoding, sight word instruction, and spelling—in ways that haven't necessarily been done before.

Chapter 2 clarifies two scientifically established pathways for literacy that have caused confusion for years. And if you are one of the thousands of kindergarten through sixth grade or special education teachers who have been fed conflicting stories about how to teach reading, as most of us have, you'll find comfort in seeing how the sounding out pathway and the orthographic, word pathway actually work together. Chapter 2 will help reading teachers at all levels understand real, scientifically grounded integrated word study based on children's early developmental levels and beyond. This chapter on the science of reading will crank up your thinking about how to meet kids where they are and move them forward as readers. You'll learn why science says all word study and reading instruction components lead to a single desirable outcome: brain words that enable reading proficiency.

CHAPTER 3
The Reading Brain

. . . clarifies and provides insight into what we know about how reading really works. We'll show you an anatomical overview of the human brain and outline its reading circuit in a way that's easy to understand and apply to your knowledge of the reading process. You don't need to be a neuroscientist to understand how to teach reading. But it does help to know about new giant leaps in science—some within the last couple of years—regarding how the reading brain works. We'll help you put it all together as a backdrop for developing brain-based representations for reading. Chapters 2 and 3 give the foundation for the practical applications presented in the chapters that follow—the stuff you can take back to your classroom with the confidence to know when, what, why, and, most importantly, how to use it.

CHAPTER 4
What Works and What Doesn't: A Critical Look at Current Teaching Practices

. . . helps you see some of the mistakes we may be making without even knowing it. With a backdrop of science, Chapter 4 investigates why some current teaching philosophies and practices fall short when it comes to building brain words—and therefore are not the best practices for developing readers. Because our science-based critique is grounded in how the brain works, as opposed to popular trends, you'll see these same concerns across all levels.

- Using instructional approaches that are not rooted in science or compatible with developmental and brain imaging research

- Assuming children will magically learn to read from mere exposure to print

- Not taking phonics to a deeper level of learning (treating phonics instruction for reading but not for spelling as sufficient) or forgetting to integrate it with other components of reading teaching

- Treating the two pathways to reading as if they were completely disconnected

- Treating decodable words and sight words as if they are learned differently (This is one of the biggest myths of reading instruction!)

- Failing to begin with an aural component that connects to the child's language system

- Failing to recognize that spelling and reading share brain processes and representations and that spelling can be used to establish brain words used in reading

- Failing to connect the auditory, spoken, and visual systems of language to word study and spelling lessons in second through sixth grade

- Misrepresenting "integrated word study" as pulling words from a reading program as opposed to building *brain words* through intentional brain-based developmentally appropriate teaching

CHAPTER 5
Phase Observation for Early Spelling to Read

. . . highlights the importance of being aware of developmental phases in best practices for teaching reading and spelling. Here we further explain the role of developmental spelling in learning to read and how spelling and reading develop in concert throughout five observable phases. You'll see how spelling and reading rely on much of the same underlying knowledge while helping to build the child's first brain words. We'll investigate kid writing and explore a variety of practical assessments to see how reading and spelling develop as two sides of the same coin. Along with that, we'll share practical examples of what you can expect to see happening concurrently as kindergarten through first- and beginning-second-grade readers and writers develop and how this information can be used to guide your teaching.

A goal of Chapter 5 is to make defining and observing Ehri and Gentry's five developmental phases easy for you and practical for classroom use. You'll see how to juxtapose all five spelling phases with expected ranges of leveled text, get tips for scaffolding invented spelling, and see how the alphabetic principle and phonics development are enhanced by scaffolding invented spelling. We will guide you through easy-to-use and time-saving formative assessment such as the Monster Test for tracking individual progress that complement whatever reading assessments you are currently using, be they running records or standardized tests or district assessments.

CHAPTER 6
Spell-to-Read: Building Brain Words in Kindergarten and First Grade

. . . outlines the basic premise of the core tenet of our approach to rethinking reading instruction and word study—a spell-to-read instructional method. Our spell-to-read teaching method is powerful for all beginning readers as well as developing readers at any grade level. It incorporates both decoding and orthographic pathways in one of the most important aspects of our book, a template for integrating reading teaching and word study to include phonological awareness, phonics, decoding, encoding, and sight words in a science-based integrated lesson. Specific teaching sequences and examples are provided.

CHAPTER 7

Building Brain Words in Second Through Sixth Grade

. . . expands on concepts presented in earlier chapters while taking second- through sixth-grade teachers back into their comfort zone. We'll provide tools for weekly word study lessons including self-testing, how questions, why questions, mixed practice, and distributed practice. We will also invite you to reconsider five traditional best practices that are newly supported by current research but often abandoned in schools today.

CHAPTER 8

Understanding and Supporting Children with Dyslexia in Light of Reading Science

. . . explores our understanding of dyslexia through the lens of the scientific study of reading presented throughout the book. Dyslexia is the most common learning disability, and the science of reading is essential to our current understanding of what it is, how to recognize the symptoms, and how best to work with students at risk of dyslexia. In this chapter we look at early intervention, indicators that classroom teachers can look for at different age and grade levels, and how to create effective accommodations for students at risk of dyslexia in the classroom.

Rethinking how we teach reading through the lens of the science of reading is critical for all of us involved with children and the teaching of reading—from the beginnings in kindergarten and first grade, through second grade and beyond, as well as children with special needs such as those at risk of dyslexia. Word reading and the establishment of lasting brain words are the focus of this book because they are in fact the link that has been missing. Building brain words and a brain dictionary enables your students to map the words on the page to a rich spoken language system. This gets them started early as readers for building concepts and vocabulary; early successes build motivation to read and write often. We can teach literacy better if we bridge the gap between the science of reading and how reading is taught in our classrooms by using the evidence-based tools in this book.

We hope you share our passion to better understand what the scientific study of reading has to say about how children learn to read and how best to help them on this journey. Our overall goal is that this book will transform your classroom by helping you rethink reading instruction and word study as a way to build an automatic and accessible dictionary in each child's brain and use the evidence-based tools we offer to enhance your teaching toward this goal. In doing so, we hope to uncover many of the questions you have about best practices for teaching reading and give you confidence as a reading and writing teacher in recognizing what works, what doesn't, and why.

CHAPTER 2

 How the Scientific Study of Reading Can Inform Teaching

As skilled readers, we are able to quickly and accurately recognize printed words without much effort. Indeed, you are most likely finding it no real chore to read this text now, and it has thus far taken only seconds of your time. You are literally matching the words on this page with *spelling* images that have been mapped or stored in your brain; these stored representations of spelling patterns, syllables, and words, linked by neural circuits to sound and meaning in your spoken language system, are what we refer to as *brain words*. Skilled reading is so efficient that you aren't even aware that you are using these stored *spellings* because it happens in such a seemingly automatic way. That is the power of brain words! By storing spelling patterns, syllables, and accurately spelled words in our internal dictionary in our brain and linking these spellings to pronunciation and meaning, we can excel in reading and writing, opening the door to a world of literacy.

When children first begin down the pathway to becoming literate, the task of word reading is often far from the automatic or effortless one just described. They don't yet have a dictionary in the brain of these spelling images. Brain words are not yet dominant in their developing brain. This is because the connections between syllable and word spelling, sound, and meaning have yet to be established; the brain's reading circuit is not yet up and fully running.

Difficulties in learning to read emerge early, and individual differences in early reading tend to remain stubbornly stable across grades. This is, of course, well documented and witnessed firsthand by teachers everywhere. Many children struggle to acquire foundational skills (National Assessment of Educational Progress 2017),

In the Classroom
Developing Brain Words

Many kindergarten and first-grade teachers use the "for-with-by" gradual release technique to assist students in reading beginner-level texts before they have established the reading skills and brain words to do so independently. First the teacher reads a selection "for" the child with fluency and slightly exaggerated expression while pointing to each word as it is said. The same selection is then read "with" the student or in a group setting with all students repeating it over and over. Eventually, the material is read "by" the student independently. The for-with-by gradual release technique is effective in helping students begin to notice the connection between print and pronunciation as they are exposed to spelling patterns that can eventually become brain words. Note that although children can self-teach some brain words during the for-with-by gradual release process, don't expect *all* brain words to be learned this way. In the chapters to come you will see why and how to build brain words through explicit instruction.

and children who lag behind their peers in learning to read in first grade are at heightened risk for continued failure (Juel 1988; Lonigan, Burgess, and Anthony 2000). And, of course, for some individuals, the process of reading can remain challenging throughout life. These challenges can be linked directly to the lack of quality brain words; *quality* here refers to the accuracy of word spelling, sound, and meaning knowledge and of the connections between them (Perfetti 2007).

It is critical that we do everything in our power to start students off successfully on the pathway to literacy and help those already on their way. This is why it is so important to have instructional approaches that are truly rooted in the science of reading theory and sound research, which have much to teach us about how reading skills are acquired in development and how this learning experience can be maximized by appropriate instruction.

In this chapter we begin with a theoretical framework that scientists have used to understand how skilled reading works; skilled reading is the kind of reading you are currently using to read this page. On a practical level, theoretical frameworks such as this one help practitioners bridge the gap between science and classroom practices by helping teachers better understand the reading process. One thing that you will learn is the central role word reading plays in any skillful reading model. Importantly, we will show how two scientifically supported routes to reading that in the past you might have thought of as separate pathways, namely the "phonics" route and the "whole word" route, do in fact work together. After we inspect a theoretical model of skilled reading, we'll move to a "developmental model" showing how children learn to read in the first place. Both models and the research in this chapter and Chapter 3 will be a good foundation for helping you deliver classroom practices grounded in current research.

Decades of research in cognitive and developmental psychology have led to a greater understanding of what is involved in learning to read. We now know that reading is a complex cognitive process; it involves many complicated processing systems that must act in concert. Recent brain imaging research supports this contention by showing just how complicated and spread out the neural circuit for reading is. Reading activates areas in the brain from the back, posterior regions through to the frontal lobe, and many areas in between. We'll show you how this works in more detail in Chapter 3, but when you consider just how complex a process reading is, and how complex the brain circuit is, it is hardly surprising that so many children and even some adults struggle with reading!

What We Know: A Theoretical Framework

Let's start with word reading because the importance of word reading is frequently overlooked. All too often the focus on *literacy* at a more global level neglects the fundamental importance of word reading. Success in reading, including higher-level processing and comprehension, is dependent upon the ability to read words. Words can be recognized, or read, in different ways. Leading developmental theorists, including Linnea Ehri of City University of New York and David Share of University of Haifa, for instance, have written extensively on how children learn to read words, and they make a clear distinction between sounding out words (serial decoding) and rapid retrieval of words from memory by sight (sight word reading). Researchers and educators alike have long documented these two subgroups of readers with significant gaps between their decoding skills (using phonics for sounding out and blending) and visual word recognition (reading by whole word or sight word recognition). You have likely seen firsthand some students who appear to be stronger in one type of reading over the other.

Acknowledgment of these two distinct processes of word reading—decoding versus visual word recognition—has been around a long time. In fact, a debate over the best way to teach reading centering around these two different ways to read has raged for over one hundred years with the pendulum swinging back and forth, baffling generations of teachers and children. In what is often described as "the reading wars," opposing factions—the decoding group, recently known as "phonics-first," and the visual word recognition group, often associated with "whole language" or "whole word instruction"—both declare their approach best for teaching all children to read. What we now know from the science of reading can lead us out of many decades of internecine battle between opposing factions.

This differentiation between decoding (phonics) and visual word recognition (sight word reading) is reflected in models of skilled reading from cognitive science. Dual-route models of skilled word reading are descriptive models that account for how word reading proceeds via two possible routes or pathways. As you will see next, the dual-route model includes a sublexical route (focused on units smaller than a word) that involves a serial letter-sound conversion *and* a lexical or orthographic route that recognizes words as wholes (Coltheart 2005; Coltheart et al. 2001)—in other words, two routes to reading.

TERMINOLOGY TACKLED:

Lexical and Sublexical

Sublexical serial decoding is what readers do when they decode a word using phonics or chunks of phonics patterns to "sound out" the word from beginning sounds moving on through to the ending sounds. It's called sublexical because it involves breaking the word or lexicon into its smaller parts. A lexicon is the stock of words in a language. *Lexical* therefore refers to whole words, and *orthography* refers to the whole word's spelling. A dual-route model includes both sublexical (phonics) and lexical/ orthographic/whole word, sometimes called "sight word," components. Both routes are needed for proficient reading.

Our simplified depiction of a dual-route model for skilled reading is shown in Figure 2.1 with the sounding out, phonics-type pathway on the left and the whole word, orthographic pathway on the right. Note that both pathways end up in the same place, in so far as the word is read by eventually linking speech sounds to the print. In the model depicted in Figure 2.1, the two routes to reading end up in what is termed the "output buffer." It's like a storing place or location in memory where data are stored before they are activated. The output buffer corresponds to an area in the brain where speech sounds are sequenced and readied for production, whether it's

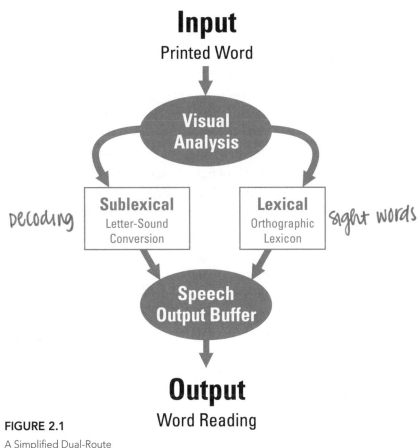

FIGURE 2.1

A Simplified Dual-Route
Model of Skilled Reading

for speech production for when you read aloud or in the form of what are often thought of as internal pronunciations in your head when you read silently. What started as print on the page ends up as speech sounds in the final "buffer" system after being processed by both routes. Scientists have proposed other connectionist models of word reading including the popular triangle model of reading, but for our discussion it's important to point out that all of them incorporate word recognition via both serial decoding (letter-sound conversion) and whole word, sight reading, just like in the two boxes in Figure 2.1 (e.g., Harm and Seidenberg 2004; Plaut et al. 1996).

It is important to be reminded that the dual-route model is a model of adult, skilled reading. It's what you are doing now because your reading circuitry is already in place. It should not be interpreted as a model of beginning reading development, which we will discuss later. This model does not in any way imply that the letter-sound route is sufficient by itself or that the whole word route to reading makes learning to read as easy as learning to speak. Furthermore, it doesn't imply that these routes to reading are always present as distinct pathways across development, nor does it mean that phonics versus whole word/ whole language approaches to word reading are in competition or need be taught in different ways. These are mistaken interpretations that have been propagated within education for decades.

KEYPOINT

As you will see, bringing the whole word visual recognition route and the letter-sound conversion route together is a critical missing piece of instruction for making learning to read easier and more efficient through children's acquisition of brain words. Remember, brain words are stored representations of spelling patterns, syllables, and words, linked by neural circuits to sound and meaning in a readers' spoken language system.

Our developmental model for beginning readers presented later in this chapter will show you what is missing in the skilled reading model shown in Figure 2.1, namely, a clear depiction of how the two routes work together and how they are actually intertwined in both early and later development and united in the process of creating brain words for literacy success. How the two routes work together for building brain words is the key piece of information missing from current approaches to teaching reading. It's what this book is all about.

Let's dig a little deeper. The two types of word reading—decoding (phonics) and visual word recognition (sight word reading)—rely on specific knowledge systems and levels of internal representations stored in the brain. Models of reading must show how the printed words connect to the sound system of a language, which is called its "phonology." This is what is happening in the final output word reading box in Figure 2.1. When engaged in serial decoding or "sounding out" a word, letters are associated with individual speech sounds, a process sometimes called letter-sound associations or phonics, where a reader must learn to map specific letters to individual phonemes or sounds. The beginning reader, struggling to sound out a word such as *fat* or *hat* letter by letter is leaning heavily on the serial letter-sound conversion reading route. In attempting to sound out the word, she may initially produce a slow and halting dysfluent pronunciation attempt such as /h/-/ă/-/t/; this will improve each time the child encounters the word.

Contrast this slow letter-by-letter process with visual word recognition or sight word reading, where the focus shifts to recognizing the word or syllable automatically using *orthography*—the symbols of spelling used to put a language into writing and the rules that govern the spellings of printed words. Sight word reading involves recognizing longer and longer strings of letters and whole word spelling or orthography. Beginners eventually move to a phase where, after several encounters with *fat* or *hat* in print, they can learn the "chunk" *at* and retrieve its pronunciation rapidly after adding the beginning sound for *f* or *h*. Eventually they can recognize *fat* and *hat* almost instantly as whole words. So recognizing the *at* chunk and retrieving it to spell an –*at* word is a *deeper* level of phonics knowledge than simply decoding. It is important to note that although recognizing the *at* chunk is part of the "orthographic" pathway, phonology is still critical to get to this deep level of recognition. But rather than letter-sound association as with decoding, orthography is more like sound-letter association as the reader matches stored sound patterns to the visual letters and words. Researcher Louisa Moats puts it this way, "Although many phonics programs and assessments speak of 'letter-sound' correspondences, the mapping system between sounds and symbols in English is more accurately conceptualized the other way around—as a map between phonemes (sounds) and graphemes (the letters that spell those sounds)." (Moats 2005/2006, 17). This mapping between sounds and graphemes is essentially what happens when we create brain words. It's about learning conventional spellings to be stored for later use in reading and writing.

KEYPOINT

It is important to point out that a word's orthography, linked to sound and meaning, is what we call a brain word—a spelling pattern that is stored in the brain. We now know that for reading, spelling patterns stored in the brain are a very big deal. If the child can spell a word correctly, she likely can read it with comprehension!

Debates concerning reading instruction, such as the reading wars where the argument is whether decoding (phonics) or sight word reading should be prioritized, are in essence outdated debates arguing if the focus should be on one route to reading or the other. Indeed, instructional approaches still tend to target one type of reading route over the other, mistakenly treating the pathways as completely disconnected and as separate teaching targets. Understanding both skilled reading and the developmental models will help you see what many educators have missed in the past: that the two routes to reading are actually intertwined in development, working together to create brain words, and hence shoud be integrated in reading instruction.

In the United States the influential report from the federal government's National Reading Panel (National Institute of Child Health and Human Development 2000), consistent with many state standards, focused on five big ideas for early literacy: phonological awareness, phonics, vocabulary, fluency, and comprehension. There should have been *six* big ideas! Notice that phonological awareness and phonics were included, but *spelling*—which we now know is explicitly involved in bringing the routes to reading together, leading directly to the storage of orthographic representations or brain words—was overlooked. Today few state standards specify clear expectations for what students at each grade level should know or be able to do in regard to spelling. And these reports and standards fail to integrate the two pathways to reading in their teaching recommendations. The same trends hold forth in Canadian schools. Yet, current research disputes this widespread practice of emphasizing only decoding but ignoring encoding or spelling and questions the wisdom behind teaching decoding and sight words separately and in completely different ways.

Developmental Theory: Linking the Routes to Reading

Having discussed a model of skilled reading, let's now see what developmental theory adds to the picture. As discussed previously, dual-route models of reading are not developmental models. Instead they describe skilled reading. In contrast, developmental theory, based on empirical evidence, describes what happens across development. In other words, how do children get to skilled reading as represented in the dual-route reading architecture shown in Figure 2.1?

Well, when we examine leading developmental theory, we can see just how these different routes to word reading intersect in development. In virtually all leading theories of how children learn to read, the initial process is proposed to be one based on phonology and decoding and not whole word or whole language. Though we do recognize that a few words such as environmental print are picked up as sight words, a focus on learning whole words without connection to processing sounds and letters is not supported by science as the best way to teach reading. In fact, to do so would be counter to what we know about the reading brain and how it changes across development.

When young children are first learning to read and spell, the initial process is based on phonology and decoding and, yes, this can be slow and laborious. As kids apply their growing knowledge and awareness of the alphabet, letters are sounded out and blended together in serial decoding of printed text, a process that consumes considerable cognitive resources. Matching individual sounds with letters during spelling can also be time-consuming and fraught with error. Think of the end-of-kindergarten child who is attempting to spell *elephant*. You can literally hear the child say the sounds out loud one after the other and try to come up with a letter to spell the sound, as in *l* for /el/, *e* for /ē/, *f* for the first sounds of the last syllable, and then perhaps *u* and *t*. *Lefut* is a common invented spelling for *elephant* at this phase of development.

Much developmental research has focused on this early entry into learning to read and spell, and our knowledge of the importance of the alphabet and awareness of speech sounds (phonological awareness) has grown exponentially as a result. We now have ample evidence that alphabetic knowledge and phonological awareness, particularly the awareness of sounds within words, are causally related to both early decoding and spelling. In other words, directly teaching the alphabet and phonological awareness helps children learn to read and spell words (Bus and van IJzendoorn 1999; Ehri et al. 2001b).

Yet, as children become more adept at reading, they begin to recognize more words rapidly and with seemingly little conscious effort. When spelling, they can reproduce syllable and word patterns just as easily. There thus seems to be a *transition on the pathway to literacy,* generally toward the end of first grade, where children progress from sounding out words letter by letter to being able to more readily recognize and spell printed text, a transition where the reading routes come together and a shift is made from one to the other. Reading is often described as becoming more automatic, more fluent, and taking far less effort. This in turn frees cognitive resources by reducing the memory load, allowing the child to focus on higher-level functions such as comprehension. As described eloquently in the oft-cited "simple view of reading" (Gough and Tunmer 1986), reading comprehension is foremost dependent upon successful word recognition. This transition on the pathway to literacy is where the routes to reading come together and brain words take over.

The acquisition of word recognition skills leading to this transition in development has been described in great detail by Linnea Ehri (1997; 2015), and you've no doubt seen this progression with your own students. According to Ehri, once children begin to associate letters with sounds, they only use some of the letters in print to read a word. For instance, children may only remember and use the *b* and *r* to read *beaver*. These children would then confuse words with similar letters; if they have learned *beaver* by cuing on the *b* and *r* and see the word *baker*, they would likely call it "beaver" in this phase (Ehri and Wilce 1987). As students master letter-sound correspondences, including vowels, they enter into a full-alphabetic level of reading where unfamiliar words can be sounded out letter by letter. In this phase beginners match a sound to each letter so that the unknown word *mat* is decoded as /m/ + /ă/ + /t/. An attempt to sound out the word *interesting* might result in /ĭ/+/n/+/t/+/ĕ/+/r/+/ĕ/+/s/+/t/+/ĭ/+/n/+/g/ mapping a sound to each letter.

Finally, Ehri proposes that word reading goes through a consolidated-alphabetic phase, where the child begins to store longer chunks of letter strings in memory. For example, the two letters of *at* may be consolidated into one chunk /ăt/, making for easy analogizing from *mat* to *cat*, *hat*, *fat*, and *sat*. In this phase the eleven

In the Classroom

The Transition on the Pathway to Literacy Witnessed

First-grade teachers often report how slow and laborious reading seems to be in the beginning phases, but often after first graders come back to school from the midyear holidays, all of a sudden fluent reading kicks in for many kids. That transition on the pathway to literacy seems like magic, but it actually coincides with the phase where first graders are now able to create many more brain words. With kids who go through the phases earlier, the "magic" happens sooner!

letters of *interesting* may be consolidated into four chunks: *in-ter-est-ing*. These chunks of letters and corresponding sounds are stored in memory leading to (orthographic) representations at the syllable and eventually whole word level, allowing for so-called sight word reading (Bhattacharya and Ehri 2004). In essence, beginning readers become more adept at storing longer and longer letter strings, or spelling patterns, in memory as they gain experience with printed words.

The take-home message here is that word reading progresses from decoding to sight word recognition as more and more orthographic representations of the spellings of syllable chunks and words are stored in the reader's brain. These are brain words and they don't magically appear—they are learned as children progress in development and the routes to reading become truly interconnected. Explicit teaching instruction based on what we know of reading and spelling development can greatly aid in this process.

The emergence of accurate spelling undergoes a similar progression, as described in detail by Richard Gentry (1982). The Ehri phases of reading acquisition and the Gentry phases of spelling development were developed independently, yet are perfectly aligned in describing the parallel development of word reading and spelling. Once more, although the earliest phases of reading and spelling reflect reliance on phonologically based processes (sounding out to hear sounds in words and matching sounds and letters), orthographic knowledge (learned spelling patterns) becomes increasingly important as reading and spelling skills develop and the learner begins to rely on longer and longer strings of letters, stored in memory as chunks and eventually whole words. These are the spelling representations stored in the brain—the

In the Classroom

Phases of Development Witnessed

Understanding the closely aligned phases of both Ehri and Gentry can help teachers detect problems and target instruction. Katrina, a third-grade teacher, noticed that one of her students was reading *over* as *even* and *cozy* as *crazy*. These kinds of mistakes are expected in Ehri's word reading and Gentry's early first-grade writing phases but not in third grade. Third graders should be chunking words in syllables for both reading and writing. Mistakes like these are signals to a teacher to have a closer look at what this student is doing and to provide intervention and target instruction for establishing fully accurate brain words.

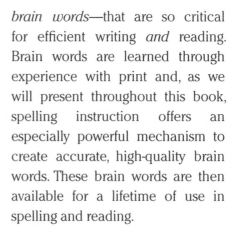

In the Classroom

The Routes to Reading and Word Walls

Word walls (classroom displays of frequently used words) are commonly used in kindergarten and first grade. It's important to remember that word walls should address both decoding (phonics) and visual word recognition (sight word reading) pathways for reading and not just be used on the false premise that students will magically learn to read through osmosis. One way to do this is to highlight word wall words that exhibit salient patterns or whatever phonics element is being taught at that time. Some teachers use transparent yellow tape for highlighting the target chunks. For example, whenever a word wall word has a common spelling chunk for a rime such as /-ăck/ and /-ăt/ in *back* and *hat*, the word can be highlighted, along with others that contain the same pattern, signaling that other words are spelled this way by analogy (Feldgus, Cardonick, and Gentry 2017).

brain words—that are so critical for efficient writing *and* reading. Brain words are learned through experience with print and, as we will present throughout this book, spelling instruction offers an especially powerful mechanism to create accurate, high-quality brain words. These brain words are then available for a lifetime of use in spelling and reading.

The transition that children make as they progress down the pathway to literacy relates directly to how the brain integrates the different routes that can be followed in reading and spelling. As children become more proficient in both reading and spelling, they lean more on the lexical or orthographic, whole word pathway, *but this route is very much dependent upon success with decoding or sounding out words*, which in turn relies on knowing the alphabet and having strong phonological awareness. The routes to reading do not develop or function in isolation. And as we will see in the next chapter, although brain imaging research has shown separate brain regions to be responsible for letter-sound decoding and whole word reading, the emergence of the latter neural circuit for word recognition is very much connected to the functioning of the former circuit for decoding (e.g., Dehaene and Cohen 2011). More on this in Chapter 3.

Developmental theory not only details a transition from sounding out words to recognizing and reproducing syllable and whole word spellings but also shows how developing brain words in the final phases are very much dependent upon earlier phases involving phonological decoding and sounding out skills. This connection between sounding out processes and syllable/word recognition has been detailed in the writings and work of renowned psychologist David Share (e.g., 2004) and his self-teaching hypothesis for orthographic learning has informed our work.

The Self-Teaching Hypothesis

David Share's self-teaching hypothesis proposes that it is the initial phonologically based sounding out of words (i.e., decoding practice) that allows children to match print with oral language, and this is what leads to the storage of word-specific representations for use in reading and writing. In essence, children teach themselves whole words and spelling patterns through experiences with sounding out print. This process of storing word-specific patterns or spelling representations is referred to as *orthographic learning* and has been proposed to play a critical role in the transition to more fluent reading and accurate spelling. Orthographic learning is the mechanism that explains the transition into Ehri's and Gentry's more advanced phases of reading and spelling development. It is the very mechanism that links the routes to reading in development. It is the very mechanism that creates brain words.

Other research has shown that orthographic learning is directly related to phonology and decoding (sounding out) skills (e.g., Cunningham et al. 2002; Ouellette and Fraser 2009); once more, this highlights the integration of the routes to reading. Moreover, research from Gene's lab has also shown that spelling practice offers even greater opportunities for self-teaching and orthographic learning as children actively explore the relations between sounds and spelling, bringing together sounding out skills and knowledge of word and syllable spellings (Ouellette and Tims 2014; Ouellette 2010).

The take-home message for teachers from all of this is a critically important one: Reading instruction need not favor one reading route over the other. Indeed, the development of the more efficient orthographic pathway depends largely upon the functioning of the more laborious sublexical, decoding route. In other words, the scientific study of reading indicates that it would be most beneficial to *integrate the two reading routes in instruction*. In this view, sounding out and blending is not only for highly consistent letter combinations; rather, these phonologically based skills are important for all word types (i.e., both regular and irregular pattern words) and for establishing, and linking, both routes to reading. Even so-called exception words are stored in memory by the same processes that are used to learn the most basic of decodable words. Likewise, *sight word reading is not just for irregular or high-*

frequency words; rather, the goal of reading instruction should be to make all words sight words! And as we will soon see, teaching reading through spelling is a science-supported way to do just this.

An Integrated Scientifically Based Model for Beginning Reading

The decades old practice of separating decoding and sight word instruction in teaching is not consistent with the developmental theory just presented. To show how teaching can align with developmental theory and integrate the routes to reading to maximize the learning of brain words, we present our own model that explicitly depicts the links between development and teaching.

Our integrated, scientifically based model for beginning reading is presented in Figure 2.2. Rather than present the routes to reading as separate pathways, we more accurately depict them here as overlapping circles. The circle on the left represents the sounding out process associated with the decoding route to reading; the circle on the right depicts the use of word and spelling patterns associated with the orthographic or

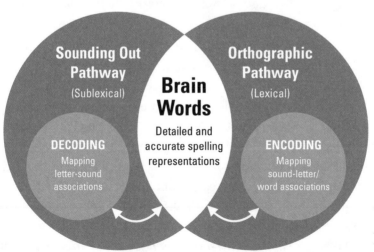

FIGURE 2.2

An Integrated Model for Beginning Reading

whole-word reading route. By representing these as overlapping circles, we make explicit the connection between the routes and the interdependencies between them as just reviewed. Of note, the overlapping middle section of the diagram represents orthographic learning and the most efficient reading—the use of brain words.

What's Meaning Got to Do with It?

It is important to remember that when we learn and store spelling in the brain, when we create brain words, these become linked to sound (i.e., pronunciation) and also to meaning. We use our preexisting knowledge—that is, our oral vocabulary—to anchor the spelling and pronunciation into memory. Charles Perfetti, a notable cognitive science researcher, describes this process as one of developing "lexical quality" (Perfetti 2007); here, *quality* refers to the accuracy of stored information for the spelling, the pronunciation, and the meaning and of the integrity of the connections between these components of word identity. And successful reading comes from having high lexical quality.

When we encounter a new word in print, we need to store all three components; there needs to be attention directed to the spelling, the pronunciation, and the meaning. Consider how much less complicated we can make the process if we already know the word. If we already know the word, we already have the meaning and pronunciation in memory—we just need to add the spelling and voilà—a brain word is established. In teaching reading our goal is to create brain words, and this can be helped along by making sure the students know the proper pronunciation and full meaning of taught words. Then we can help them add the spelling knowledge so that they can then rapidly read and accurately write these words.

⚙ Research in Action

How Naming the Lab Cat *Yait* Made a Nonsense Word Easier to Learn and Other Lessons from the Lab

Orthographic learning researchers often use a paradigm in which students are exposed to nonwords and then are evaluated on how well they can recognize and spell the "words." Nonwords are used to avoid any effects of prior word knowledge, and the patterns chosen are ambiguous in the sense that they could be spelled in more than one way. For example, the child may be exposed to a spelling such as *yait* or *yate* (the pronunciation of each would be the same). To later recognize or recreate the correct spelling for this newly taught "word," the learner needs to establish an orthographic representation or brain word; if they rely only on decoding and phonics knowledge, they would not know which phonologically permissible spelling would be the "correct" one. In one research study, Gene added a twist—definitions and pictures were created for some of the nonwords. For example, a *yait* was presented as a catlike animal that lived in a garden in New York City. Results showed that students were able to more accurately learn and store the new spellings when the nonwords were given meaning, showing the importance of integrating phonology (sound), orthography (spelling), and meaning (Ouellette and Fraser 2009).

The Missing Piece: The Connection Between Spelling and Reading

Up to this point, we've discussed research that highlights how decoding or sounding out words is important in orthographic learning and in establishing brain-based syllable and word representations. Yet as alluded to earlier, research by Gene and others (Ouellette and Tims 2014; Ouellette 2010; Shahar-Yames and Share 2008) has shown that *spelling practice is even more effective than decoding experiences in establishing these spelling patterns in the brain.*

Most instructional approaches treat reading and spelling as two totally separate skills; yet this is not actually the case. In fact, recent work by Gene and his colleague and mentor Monique Sénéchal has further highlighted the importance of developmental spelling in learning to read (Ouellette and Sénéchal 2017; Ouellette, Sénéchal, and Haley 2013; Ouellette and Sénéchal 2008). These researchers have convincingly shown that having children practice spelling words is a great way to teach reading. But note, this does not mean merely asking students to memorize a spelling list; it means starting out by having them listen to a word and then to try to come up with the spelling on their own followed by a scaffolded discussion about their invented spelling, eventually comparing that attempt to the correct spelling.

Throughout this process, the teacher relies on the developmental phases of reading and writing to nudge the child to higher phases. This spell-to-read approach is detailed in Chapter 6 where we outline a number of specific activities and techniques for teachers to use with beginning readers. In Chapter 7 you will see how this method can be used in second grade and beyond.

 Research in Action

How Spelling *Yait* Created a New Brain Word

In another study teaching young students new "words" like *yait*, Gene had some students practice the new words by repeatedly reading them; others practiced by spelling them (Ouellette 2010). Guess who learned the most new words? If you guessed the students who practiced spelling you would be correct! The sound-to-letter matching process of spelling benefits orthographic learning and anchors the spelling, sound, and meaning connections in long-term memory. This is, in essence, how brain-based spelling representations—our brain words—are formed.

Other research reiterates that spelling practice transfers to reading improvement in general, far more so than reading practice alone transfers to spelling improvement. Recent meta-analyses have shown that spelling instruction benefits word reading across the school years (Graham and Hebert 2011), most specifically in the elementary years (Graham and Santangelo 2014). Research from cognitive psychology, including a recent study conducted by Gene, Sandra Martin-Chang, and Maya Rossi (2017), has shown that older readers are able to read words they can spell more quickly than they can read words they cannot spell; this confirms that spelling accuracy reflects the quality of the brain-based representation for a word. And higher-quality, more accurate brain-based spelling representations equal better reading.

The Spell-to-Read Advantage: An Integrated Approach for Teaching Reading

Our spell-to-read teaching method is a research-based, developmentally aligned approach that links hearing, speech, language, and vision and is an analytic process that helps connect the auditory (phonology) to the visual (orthography) and to the meaning in establishing brain words. Starting with a child-generated spelling attempt and progressing to the accurate brain-based spelling, instruction is matched to the individual student. The word is then used in reading and writing activities to help the child continue to develop an accurate brain-based representation (i.e., *brain word*), that is to say, the correct spelling for the word, that links phonology, orthography, and meaning and essentially *integrates the routes to reading*.

Based on scientific research, a spell-to-read methodology for teaching word reading gives teachers an advantage for successfully teaching beginning readers. Foremost it enables teachers to link the two scientifically established pathways for literacy, the sounding out pathway and the orthographic pathway, that heretofore have been treated as separate pathways for teaching beginners. In doing so, it enables teachers to maximize the learning of brain words. This is true scientifically based *integrated reading instruction* with techniques that incorporate phonological awareness, decoding, encoding, and sight word recognition into a single instructional approach rather than treating each of these essential elements of learning to read as standalone instruction.

In Figure 2.3, we present our integrated model again, but this time we include instructional methods connected to the aspects of reading they are matched to. Our intent here is to allow you to see (A) how the routes to reading overlap and come together, and (B) how reading instruction can be altered to prioritize the creation and use of brain words. This is the crux of our spell-to-read approach to teaching word reading, described in detail in later chapters.

Our integrated model for beginning reading shows how the two formerly separated pathways and knowledge systems for beginning readers can now be brought together in a single scientifically based conceptualization. In the past the sounding out pathway and the orthographic (or sight word) pathway were envisioned as two separated routes, each representing a competing approach. Here we have brought them together to show how today's science supports linking the two pathways to develop accurate and efficient word reading—for all words. Importantly Figure 2.3 demonstrates how six instructional beginning reading techniques that formerly were treated as stand-alone instruction—namely, phonological awareness instruction, phonics instruction, isolated word study, word wall exposure, whole language word study, and other isolated sight word exposures such as word sorts—can now all be incorporated into one more efficient and effective *integrated* approach to teaching reading that is developmentally appropriate and scientifically valid. On a practical level, it's critical to teach spelling—something that has not been emphasized in many schools for over two decades.

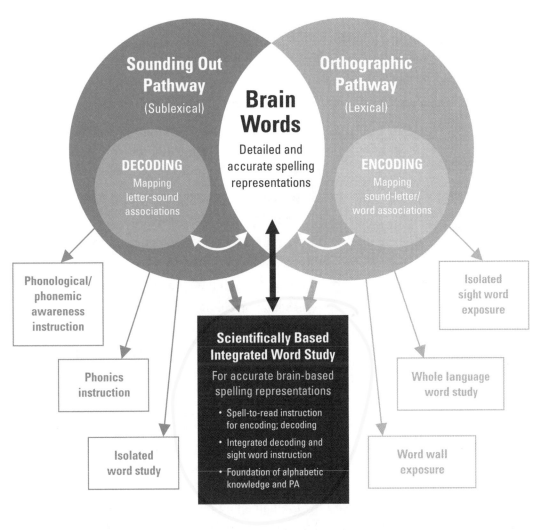

FIGURE 2.3

An Integrated Model for Beginning
Reading with Teaching Applications

Notice how the interlinking section of the model's Venn diagram represents the ultimate goal of reading instruction for all beginning readers and for all word types: building a store of detailed and accurate spelling representations in each child's brain. This "dictionary in the brain" of correct spellings (i.e., *brain words*) can then be used for a lifetime of automatically recognizing the learned words for reading and automatically retrieving them for writing, thereby freeing the brain for comprehension and meaning making. This is the focus of our spell-to-read approach and often the missing link to effective literacy instruction.

In this chapter we summarized reading theory and research that show:

KEYPOINT

The ultimate goal of word study for all beginning readers and for all word types is to build a store of detailed and accurate spelling representations in each child's brain—that is, to establish brain words. Continuing to add brain words through explicit systematic spelling instruction also extends beyond second grade to help achieve reading proficiency at higher grade levels.

A. Descriptively, there are two routes or pathways to word reading utilizing different forms of representations or knowledge systems.

B. These pathways are intertwined and interdependent in development.

C. Care should be taken to integrate these pathways during reading instruction.

D. Word reading benefits from high-quality representations in the brain—for spelling, pronunciation, and meaning.

E. Spelling can be used to teach reading, establish brain-based spelling representations, integrate the routes to reading, and lead to more efficient word reading for all word types.

This chapter presents the "what" and "why" behind rethinking reading instruction to bring our teaching practices in line with developmental theory and research. This is precisely how the scientific study of reading can inform teaching. In the next chapter, we will see how brain-imaging research aligns remarkably well with the developmental theory and research just presented, lending further scientific backing to our spell-to-read approach to teaching reading. We then turn our attention to exploring how knowledge of this science of reading can be used to reevaluate how we may currently be teaching reading (Chapter 4).

Taken together, these chapters bridge the gap between what science says about the teaching of reading and best practices for the classroom along with tips for meeting the needs of children who struggle. Understanding the science of reading will show you how to teach reading in ways that are more effective than what we have been doing in the past.

CHAPTER 3

 The Reading Brain

In this chapter we present an overview of how the reading brain works. Our current knowledge of the reading brain comes from decades of research that employs various techniques used to directly observe brain activity during reading. With recent advancements in technology, scientists have been able to more clearly watch the brain in action and more precisely identify brain regions involved in specific functions. As a direct result, our understanding of the reading brain has grown significantly. The culmination of this research has been the identification of what is now referred to as the *neurological reading circuit*. And just as we argued for developmental theory and reading research, this brain-imaging research can, and indeed should, inform practice when it comes to teaching reading. And—spoiler alert!—the findings from brain-imaging research align nearly perfectly with the reading theory we just presented in Chapter 2.

The Human Brain

The human brain is truly a wondrous and utterly complex thing. It is estimated to contain about 85 to 120 billion cells. The sheer magnitude of that number is difficult to even imagine: 85 to 120 billion cells! Oh, and we should add that each cell is connected to hundreds and possibly even thousands of others: it is estimated that these billions of cells have more than 160 trillion connections between them (Lilienfeld, Lynn, and Namy 2018). We end up with an organ that has been described by many as the most complex structure in the known universe. It is a structure that allows for consciousness, thought, creativity, emotion, language . . . a structure that is essentially at the core of who we are. Considering the complexity of the structure itself and the complexity of the functions it undertakes, it is hardly surprising that the precise workings of the human brain have eluded scientists for centuries.

Although each brain is unique in some way, everyone's brain has common patterns of cellular structure and organization, and these areas and pathways are related to specific functions including motor and perceptual processes. We have known for some time, for example, where many specific speech and language processes are based in the brain. With modern advancements in brain-imaging techniques, scientists continue to more precisely identify and map out specific brain regions and circuits that underlie human behavior, and this includes reading. Not surprisingly, the reading circuit in the brain appears to be an incredibly complex, interactive system that integrates various brain regions as well as perceptual and motor functions.

Reading may well be something we highly literate adults take for granted, but when you break it down, it is a multifaceted psychological process. Printed text must be perceived and processed visually; symbols must be matched to stored representations for sounds and connected to meaning; speech codes must be accessed for pronunciation; higher-order language skills need to be involved for processing sentences and for comprehension. Perhaps most astounding is that this all happens within milliseconds in proficient reading, with many of these processes seemingly happening at the same time.

KEYPOINT

Reading theory, research, and brain-imaging studies all have much to say about how reading develops and how we can best teach it. Perhaps it is time we listened.

As detailed in the previous chapter, the reading process is foremost dependent on successful word recognition or word reading. If a word cannot be read (by some means), then the reading process grinds to a halt. That is why word reading is the focus of this book and why we assert that instructional approaches must prioritize its teaching and must do so in ways that are consistent with reading theory, research, and our growing understanding of the reading brain.

Brain Organization

The outer layer of the brain is referred to as the cerebral cortex. The largest and most studied component of the human brain, the cortex is the wrinkly surface that we see when looking at pictures of the brain. It is estimated to account for approximately 80 percent of our brain's mass. Researchers believe that the wrinkled, folded topography of this outer brain layer is a result of continued cortex growth through evolution combined with the constraining size of the human skull (Pinel 2018). The result: a convoluted, folded surface, rich in brain cells and their intricate connections. The cerebral cortex is implicated in many so-called higher-order cognitive functions such as consciousness, language, and thought. And reading.

Anatomically, the cerebral cortex is divided into two halves, or hemispheres, and in each we can see four distinct lobes separated by deep fissures or clefts on the surface. This anatomical structure and organization is depicted in Figure 3.1, which shows the left hemisphere, or side of the brain, where language and reading processes are known to reside for most.

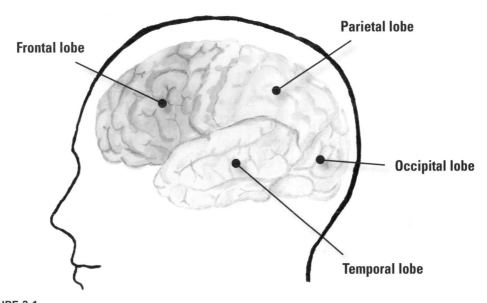

FIGURE 3.1

The Human Brain

The four discrete lobes of the brain are highly interconnected and integrated, yet each is also implicated in distinct human functions and behaviors. Although each lobe is associated with its own functions, it should be noted that all four major lobes are involved to some extent when it comes to reading (see Table 3.1). Because the neurological reading circuit is spread out over these dispersed cortical areas, it reasons then that the reading circuit is just as highly complex and interconnected as the brain itself. In other words, successful reading relies on multiple processing areas spread out across the human brain. This is a critical point to keep in mind and one that we will return to over and over as we further consider the neurological basis for reading.

TABLE 3.1

Brain Lobes and Functions

Lobe	Noted Functions	Contribution to Reading
Occipital	Visual processing	Processing letter shape; visual scanning
Parietal	Sensory processing; bodily awareness; understanding	Processing sound sequences; linkage to syntax and meaning
Temporal	Hearing/auditory processing; language; emotion	Phonemic processing; linkage to syntax and meaning
Frontal	Motor output; speech and language; thought; self-regulation	Speech planning and grammar/morphological processes

Brain Specialization: From Speech and Language to Reading

It is estimated that we have been speaking to one another for over 100,000 years, but only reading for a few thousand years (Lilienfeld, Lynn, and Namy 2018). It can be argued that our brains were not originally set up to read. Instead, most neuroscientists believe that parts of the brain, perhaps intended for other purposes, have been "recruited" for reading (Dehaene-Lambertz, Monzalvo, and Dehaene 2018). Over time, what we refer to today as the *neurological reading circuit* has evolved. Critically, the reading circuit does not appear to be present at birth; rather, it develops only with exposure and experience—first with language and then with print. Ideally these beginnings are enriched with environmental stimulation and efficacious teaching.

Many of the brain regions involved in reading are ones that are first specialized for oral speech and language processes (DeWitt and Rauschecker 2013). Indeed, we begin to develop the speech and language skills required for learning to read as infants—perhaps even earlier. The sounds we encounter, the vocalizations we make, and the human interactions we have as infants together set language acquisition and brain specialization in motion.

As infants we have an amazing ability not only to hear language but to hear fine-grained differences between speech sounds. Some of these variances between speech sounds are not even detectable by adults, but infants can hear the distinctions between nearly all sounds in nearly all languages (Werker and Tees 2002). Even more impressive perhaps is that studies have shown that we can

process the statistical properties of a language. In other words, not only do we become aware of what environmental sounds are the "speech sounds" that make up our native language but we also process the statistical probability that certain sounds occur in sequence (Kuhl et al. 2008). Take for example the sound of the digraph *th*. It is often followed by a neutral schwa vowel sound (/ə/) "uh," as in *the*, and we learn this by simply listening to language. We also learn rules such as two stop consonants (e.g., /p/ and /b/) cannot follow each other to start a word. We learn this and various other sequence constraints unique to our native language. And we do all of this before our first birthday.

Meanwhile, our early vocalizations help to prepare our vocal apparatus (including our lips, tongue, and vocal cords) for speech as we gradually develop the motor coordination needed to speak. Eventually we babble speech sounds, leading up to our first words. From there, language development really takes off, enriched by human interactions and experiences that immerse us in meaningful language. We become proficient talkers and grow in our ability to understand the language around us. By the time we start formal schooling, we have nearly mastered the sentence structure and grammar of our language. If we have had a rich stimulating environment, we can know thousands and thousands of words. Yes, thousands (e.g., Biemiller 2009).

During this developmental period, the language areas of the brain involved in language processing and production become highly specialized and interconnected (see Figure 3.2). These neural areas located chiefly in the left hemisphere of the brain form the epicenter from which the reading circuit is to be built. These major localized language centers include (Friederici 2012):

- Areas of the frontal lobe, particularly around the third inferior frontal gyrus (known as Broca's area), involved with grammatical processing and speech processing/planning/production (For example, this is where a word's pronunciation is programmed and sent out for speech production.)

- Areas of the superior and posterior temporal lobe, adjacent to the parietal lobe (including the region known as Wernicke's area), responsible for processing and storing speech sounds (For example, this is where a word's phonology or sound structure is analyzed and where representations of phonemes [speech sounds] are believed to be housed.)

- Other areas of the temporal lobe, active in semantic/syntactic processing (i.e., meaning and sentence structure) (For example, this is where sentence structures and meaning are processed.)

- Areas of the inferior parietal lobe, involved in linking temporal and frontal regions and also active in comprehension, phonological memory, and connecting sound to meaning (For example, memory processes specialized for speech sounds are thought to reside here.)

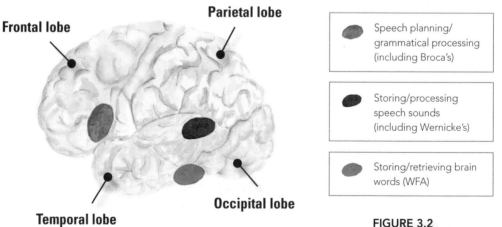

Parietal lobe

Frontal lobe

Temporal lobe

Occipital lobe

Speech planning/
grammatical processing
(including Broca's)

Storing/processing
speech sounds
(including Wernicke's)

Storing/retrieving brain
words (WFA)

FIGURE 3.2

Language Processes
in the Brain

Defining the Reading Circuit

Brain-imaging studies have repeatedly demonstrated that efficient word reading involves the dispersed reading circuit in the brain comprising the brain areas just described in the left hemisphere (Chyl et al. 2018; Waldie et al. 2017). In particular, when we decode or sound out words, areas around the junction of the parietal and temporal lobes process letter-sound conversion, and this is highly linked to the areas of the frontal lobe involved in speech processing and production (Pugh 2006). In simpler terms, when we sound out words and letters, our temporal/parietal regions light up along with the frontal speech areas—even when we read silently.

KEYPOINT

The *neurological reading circuit* foremost depends on the integration of known speech- and language-processing areas of the brain. These areas are activated through hearing and auditory processing. This is why phonological awareness is so important and why invented spelling is such a great starting point for children to match an auditory analysis with print.

But something is missing from the description and explanation offered to this point. After all, isn't reading also a visual medium? Reading involves print, and we process print through vision. So how does this critical reality of reading fit into what has thus far been a discussion of oral speech and language brain areas largely focused on hearing and phonology? Well, if you recall from Table 3.1, visual input is processed in the occipital lobe, at the back of the brain. Perhaps not the most efficient organization, but that is the way it is—visual information travels from our eyes on the front of our head all the way to the back of the brain for processing. This visual input is then fed forward and connected to the phonology-processing and sound-letter network just described.

Yet this is still not the entire story—there is one more critical piece to the puzzle of the reading brain. Neuroscientists have uncovered another brain area that appears critical for skilled, fluent reading, an area that becomes specialized during reading acquisition to specifically process and store the visual representation of print—from individual letters, to letter sequences and chunks, to whole words. This region, found along a gyrus that overlaps temporal and occipital areas, is known as the *Word Form Area*, or WFA (Dehaene and Cohen 2011; Cohen and Dehaene 2004). This can be seen designated by the red oval in Figure 3.2.

The Word Form Area is believed to house the dictionary of word patterns and spellings that a reader has been exposed to and mastered. These are our *brain words*. Critically, these brain words are used in both reading and spelling (Purcell, Jiang, and Eden 2017). This is where chunks of letters or parts of words are recognized and where detailed, brain-based syllable and word representations are stored. As Richard describes, it is where readers see a word's spelling in their mind's eye (Gentry 2004). The Word Form Area completes the reading circuit and accounts for both skilled and deficient reading. It is the brain area that appears to best distinguish strong from poor readers and has been implicated in dyslexia (Dehaene 2009).

Now, here is another critical piece of information about the reading brain: each of these areas—the frontal lobe for speech, the temporal/parietal lobe for sound representation and meaning, and the Word Form Area for spelling representations—do not in themselves bring about skilled reading. Recall that brain cells can have trillions of connections between them. Well, for the reading circuit to fully develop in the brain, these vital brain regions need to establish an intricate series of connections with each other. This is where environmental stimulation and efficacious reading instruction come in and where you as a teacher can make a huge impact. Through intentional, science-based reading instruction you can actually help the developing brain by stimulating the development of the integrated, complex reading circuit just described. In the following chapters we will provide more information on how this can be done with a spell-to-read approach to teaching word reading.

KEYPOINT

Researchers have repeatedly shown that learning to read results in observable changes to the reading brain and, in particular, to a stronger role of the Word Form Area and stronger links between the various brain regions involved in reading and writing. And this is built on a foundation of speech, language, sound-letter knowledge, and auditory/phonological processing.

The final piece of information that we must stress to complete this discussion of the reading brain is a critically important one that is often overlooked: *The reading brain changes during learning to read.* That is why the way we teach reading is so important. Researchers have queried, for example, if the Word Form Area is already a specialized, functioning center in our brain prior to becoming literate or if it emerges only as we learn to read. There is now consensus that it is in fact the latter—the Word Form Area emerges with exposure to print, as alphabetic knowledge and phonological awareness is gained, and even further as decoding skills are learned. This reflects how areas of the brain are "recruited" for reading (Dehaene and Cohen 2011); and the stimulus for this recruitment is early alphabetic, phonological awareness and decoding/encoding skills (Monzalvo and Dehaene-Lambertz 2013). What we are referring to here is the very integration of the routes to reading presented in Chapter 2. This is the neurological reality underlying how decoding and sight word reading become linked, share underlying processes, and lead to the establishment of brain words. And this is where we can look for guidance in developing the most efficacious teaching methods.

Research in Action

The Brain Responds to Reading Instruction

Neuroimaging studies have repeatedly shown changes in brain activity as children learn to read. Although there is some debate over just when the Word Form Area becomes prominent, there is a growing consensus that it emerges only as early reading skills are acquired. In a longitudinal study that analyzed brain imaging from children as they progressed from kindergarten to second grade, Maurer et al. (2006) found no specialized activation for sensitivity to letter strings in prereaders entering school, but such processing, associated with the Word Form Area, was well established by second grade. Teaching studies have also shown increased activation in the Word Form Area following targeted interventions for letter-sound correspondences and decoding (e.g., Brem et al. 2010).

Putting It All Together

Thinking back to the reading research and theory presented in Chapter 2, several parallels become readily apparent. The gradual recruitment and growing involvement of the Word Form Area can be seen as the brain changes behind David Share's self-teaching and orthographic learning and in the progressions detailed in Linnea Ehri's and Richard's phases of development. Changes seen in the developing brain are responsible for what was described in Chapter 2 as the *transition on the pathway to literacy*. Indeed, these documented changes in the reading brain can be seen as the neural manifestation of the developmental theory presented in Chapter 2. The gradual emergence of the Word Form Area reflects the integration of the routes to reading as children learn longer letter strings and whole word spelling patterns. The increasing role of the Word Form Area reflects an increased reliance on orthographic

In the Classroom

Monitoring Brain Changes

You can monitor brain changes through phase observation in kindergarten and first grade as the Word Form Area and brain words are being developed. In Chapter 5 we show you how to use phase observation to monitor and guide your students' reading and spelling progress and reading circuitry development.

KEYPOINT

A listening-first tenet is central to our spell-to-read approach for teaching brain words. Students begin with hearing when we help beginners stretch through the sounds in a word as we scaffold their invented spelling, eventually comparing it to the correct model. Older students first listen and *hear* a pretest word as we make sure students have the word's meaning in their spoken vocabulary as a key component of self-testing. This hearing-first and connecting to spoken vocabulary approach is directly in line with developmental theory and brain research and one that can help your students succeed on the pathway to literacy.

learning and brain words in more skilled reading and writing. And the links between the Word Form Area and the speech/language brain regions reflect how sight word reading is built on a foundation of decoding and phonological skills. And critically, the developmental brain changes associated with learning to read tell us that our teaching matters.

The refinement of the brain circuitry that occurs as children learn to read is perfectly compatible with our model of reading presented in Chapter 2. Recall, the sublexical, sounding out route to word reading sets the stage for the emergence of the lexical, whole word reading route. Consistent with our integrated model of word reading, these routes to reading are better envisioned in development as overlapping and interdependent processes, and this is confirmed in the brain-imaging research.

Finally, we stress one more time that the dispersed reading circuit in the brain, spread out from the visual-processing areas at the back of the brain to the speech and planning centers at the front of the brain, is highly interconnected. And this again reflects the integration of the different routes to reading. Furthermore, this highlights the importance of audition. The reading circuit begins with hearing: listening to sounds, analyzing the sounds in words, and connecting this information with print. In many ways, listening (processed in the temporal lobe) mediates the connections between vision (processed at the back of the brain) and speech (programmed at the front of the brain). That is why a spell-to-read approach is so effective in teaching students to read. By starting with an auditory analysis, rather than visual memorization, children effectively activate their reading circuitry. Through invented spelling and teacher feedback, accurate brain-based representations—brain words—can be established. Starting with auditory analysis also applies when we discuss pretesting developing spellers in second grade and beyond (see Chapter 7). Indeed, this is at the heart of our recommended spell-to-read approach to teaching word reading, as presented in detail in Chapters 6 and 7.

The conclusions derived from brain-imaging studies map onto developmental theory astonishingly well. This makes it all the more surprising that this scientific study of reading continues to be neglected in much instructional practice and leads us to the central question—how do we best teach children to read and spell words in ways that facilitate the development of a strong reading circuit in the brain? In the next chapters we review current practice and present our spell-to-read instructional approach that is built from developmental theory, behavioral research, and the current brain-imaging data.

KEYPOINT

What We've Learned So Far

1. *Word reading* is built upon a foundation of speech and oral language and is an essential outcome: if kids can't read the *words*—even in isolation—the reading process halts.

2. *Word reading* requires decoding; decoding requires the *integration* of alphabetic knowledge, phonological awareness, and phonics knowledge/skills to connect pronunciations to strings of letters in long-term memory. This integration happens in the child's brain, linking letters, sound, and meaning.

3. Though we used to think of them as competing processes associated with phonics-first versus whole language, today we know that the two routes to reading intersect in development. Efficient *word reading* requires an explicit connection between decoding and sight word reading as the Word Form Area emerges to complete the reading circuit in the brain.

4. Brain words are established through orthographic learning as the routes to reading intersect in practice and in the brain.

5. Listening, speaking, spelling, and reading share brain processes and stored representations. Listening and spelling activities integrate the reading routes and associated brain regions and lead directly to the development of brain words.

6. The developing reading circuit in the brain is distributed across lobes and must rely on a high degree of interconnectedness to function efficiently; the development of the fully functioning, highly integrated reading circuit can be facilitated by aligning our teaching with what we now know about developmental theory and brain-imaging research. This is our focus in the chapters to come.

CHAPTER 4

What Works and What Doesn't: A Critical Look at Current Teaching Practices

Independent reading depends foremost on the ability to read words. As eloquently described by Marilyn Adams (1998), "Words, as it turns out, are the raw data of text. It is the words of a text that evoke the starter set of concepts and relationships from which its meaning must be built" (73). Word reading excels when the reader can build a dictionary of brain words—precise spellings in the brain anchored to pronunciation and meaning. Brain words connect with our spoken language system, allowing us to make meaning from words on a page. Without efficient word reading—that is to say, brain words—comprehension and fluency are compromised. Without automatic spelling expertise it's very difficult to write with fluency and cogency even if the student has a high level of reasoning skill and oral expression.

The truth is that word reading proficiency and the development of automaticity using brain words, the deepest level of complete word representations in the Word Form Area of the brain, should be on the top of everyone's list when it comes to instructional goals. Yet many approaches to teaching reading do not take notice of the scientific study of reading and the brain. Building brain words is currently neither a goal of teaching nor an outcome of student learning common to many of the practices that persist in today's classrooms. In this chapter we will consider approaches and methods for teaching reading in light of current research and the scientific study of reading. Some of these may even be familiar and popular practices. We realize we will be stepping on some toes and for that we apologize, but we hope you will welcome a frank discussion of how the science of reading sheds light on why some current practices are not working. There is indeed a void between the latest research and educational practices in too many school districts; most teachers want to understand why what they are doing is not working. This chapter is about the mistakes we educators are making without knowing it and how the science of reading can help us fix them.

The gap between the scientific study of reading and teaching practice has been acknowledged for some time now—it is nothing new, but it is increasingly being highlighted as a major educational problem that can no longer be ignored (Hanford 2018; Sanchez 2018; Seidenberg 2017). We are far from the first researchers or academic writers to advocate for increasing teacher knowledge of reading science. Indeed, we are part of a growing list of professionals who stress the importance of understanding developmental theory, research, and brain study when it comes to teaching reading (e.g., Loisa Moats, Marilyn Adams, Matatesha Joshi, Steve Graham, Anne Cunningham, Mark Seidenberg). Within the scientific community there has long been a clear consensus that specialized knowledge is essential for teaching reading most effectively (e.g., Association for Childhood Education International 2007). Yet the gap between science and teaching practice stubbornly persists.

Let's not mince words; what we are pointing out is that too many teachers—even teachers who teach beginning and struggling readers—have not been properly trained to teach literacy based on the current science. It is still possible in many areas to obtain a degree and a teaching certificate as an elementary school teacher without taking a single course on reading theory and practice. And reading courses that do exist often fail to survey primary research and theory or present a fully accurate, up-to-date picture of the reading process.

Research in Action

Teaching our Teachers

Matatesha Joshi and colleagues from Texas A&M University surveyed textbooks used in teacher education programs and found that most failed to adequately cover components of effective literacy instruction, and even more troubling, many were found to present inaccurate information (Joshi et al. 2009). Studies by Anne Cunningham of the University of California, Berkeley, Catherine Snow of Harvard, and others have indeed confirmed that many teachers remain unfamiliar with the science of reading, especially in the K-2 sector (e.g., Cunningham et al. 2004).

Compounding matters, many teachers do not have access to science-based teaching resources. It's no fault of the teachers, but we do hold accountable teacher education programs; publishers who neglect to consider the science behind the products they sell; theorists and special interest groups who do the same in promoting their political agenda—whether it be phonics-first, whole language, the constructivist movement, so-called "balanced literacy," self-styled "comprehensive integrated language arts reading programs," or other educational curricula—and even a few super-authors who have allowed publishers to make them *experts in everything* to sell more products. These all may share the blame of promoting teaching without regard to the scientific study of reading itself.

We have great respect for teachers and advocate for them, especially in so many places where they feel like they are continuously being told to adopt new programs, only to be told later to throw them out and do something different. We hope a scientific look at what works and what doesn't work will help bring more consistency and continuity in what we are asking of teachers, bring better preservice training and expertise based on science, and help promote better teaching resources.

In this chapter, we show you how a better understanding of the science of reading can lead to teaching that is truly evidence- and science-based. It is through understanding developmental phases, how the routes to reading are intertwined in development, and how the Word Form Area emerges over time in the reading brain that we come to realize how simple decodable words and more difficult sight words are processed and learned in the same way, eventually becoming brain words. And we can better understand the importance of spelling in learning to read and in establishing the brain words critical for proficient word reading and easier written composition.

What We Now Know and What the National Reading Panel Left Out

Before we take a critical look at what works and what doesn't in current teaching practices, let's first reconsider what we actually know about learning to read and why a critical component of the reading process is missing in most discussions today. This missing link is most noticeably absent in the report issued by the National Reading Panel (National Institute of Child Health and Human Development 2000) that listed five essential components of reading teaching: phonological awareness, phonics, fluency, vocabulary, and comprehension. Although well intentioned and in many regards helpful, this report fell short in linking teaching with current knowledge about the importance of *learning to read words automatically*. Automatic word reading, which benefits from accurate brain words, is arguably the most important component to learning to read.

Consider this: Keith Stanovich has reported that as children build their spoken language system, they learn approximately seven new words a day (especially if they are a reader) or 3,000 words a year (as reported in Shaywitz 2003, 106). Each year in elementary school there is an opportunity for children to install the precise *spelling* of many of these words into the dictionary in their brain, along with the words' pronunciation and meaning. These brain words can then light up with the students' whole reading circuitry when encountered in print, with an outcome of comprehension. Without efficient word reading, however, the entire process grinds to a halt. In other words, without accurate word reading and a connection between stored words and children's oral speech and language system, there can be no fluency or comprehension, because both are very much based on successful word reading (Shaywitz 2003; Gough and Tumner 1986). In fact, the National Reading Panel's "fluency" and "comprehension" components can actually be seen as *outcomes* of successful word reading. And efficient word reading can be achieved with properly stored brain words.

The National Reading Panel simply left out a focus on spelling—and in doing so, it neglected orthographic learning and brain words. Perhaps this was because the report came out at a time when whole language dominated reading instruction and denigrated explicit systematic standalone spelling instruction (Dehaene 2009; Woo 1997). When the Common Core State Standards were released in 2009, the initiative had been influenced widely by the National Reading Panel; consequently, the Common Core State Standards and other standards crafted to mirror them have ignored spelling, orthographic learning, and brain words as well (Moats 2005/2006).

What Works and What Doesn't: A Critique of Teaching Practice

The swinging pendulum between whole language and phonics-first has influenced how reading has been taught for decades now. Those battles continue despite our increased knowledge of how kids learn to read and how the reading brain develops. Perhaps it is fitting then that we begin our specific critique with a critical look at whole language and phonics. We'll consider commonly used specific teaching practices and conclude with some thought of what is conspicuously missing from many of today's classrooms.

Whole Language

Today, some of the world's foremost researchers in cognitive neuroscience and reading such as Stanislas Dehaene along with many educational researchers vehemently affirm that aspects of whole language and the whole word approach lack the support of today's science. Yet we see too many of the unscientific whole language practices often called "constructivist" or by some other name persist in many classrooms. The heart of the problem is that whole language (just like phonics-first) focuses almost exclusively with one—and only one—of what we now know are *two* scientifically established intertwined brain pathways to reading. Decoding and sight word reading rely on the same underlying processes; they are integrated in practice and in the brain, and sight-word reading is built from decoding skills. But whole language approaches neglect this fact in teaching whole word reading only.

Today's science challenges many of the core tenets of whole language despite the fact that whole language practices continue to be used in many classrooms. The core problem with whole language is that the movement was largely built on the theory and promise that learning to read was as natural as learning to speak (Goodman 1986). We now know that although speaking and reading share many processing domains and brain areas, the actual brain development for reading and speaking are inherently different, and unlike oral language, the development of reading brain circuitry requires explicit instruction (see Chapters 2 and 3).

Learning to speak is natural—the human brain is wired for it—but for most children learning to read has to be explicitly taught; it's really that simple. Learning to speak a language or several languages can be "easy" if the child—particularly at a very early age—is immersed in a spoken language environment; in contrast, most children will not learn to read, write, or spell under similar circumstances because they are not born with reading circuitry. They don't learn the intricacies of written language by osmosis, inferring, picking it up, hypothesizing the rules or patterns, or figuring out how phonics and the complex English spelling system works without instruction. For most kids reading and spelling are not "caught" simply from immersion—even in a rich language environment with teacher support. They have to be taught. Despite the initial contention of whole language theorist, reading is not a "psycholinguistic guessing game" driven by meaning (Goodman 1967). As it turns out, gaining meaning is certainly important—it's the end goal of reading—but seeing and recognizing words automatically, linking to phonology, and integrating the components of reading with one's own spoken language and vocabulary are what really drive the reading process. It's not a guessing game based on meaning and syntax.

Without doubt many positive transformational changes in education were advanced by whole language such as the use of invented spelling, classrooms filled with good children's literature to motivate children to read, and the use of thematic units. It has brought us the Donald Graves and Donald Murray process writing approach and has led to more time for reading in school and a better integration of reading and writing across the curriculum.

Importantly, however, in light of what we currently know from science, the following whole language practices were in some cases devastating shortcomings and many of them persist today. Whole language teachers were told the following (Goodman 1986):

- Do not teach phonics because children will intuit phonics by reading (the National Reading Panel and Common Core have largely reversed this recommendation).

- Do not use spelling books or teach spelling explicitly and systematically. Expect children to pick up spelling skills in the context of reading and writing (spelling books are in fact supported by research: Gentry 2004; Moats 2005/2006; Wallace 2006).

- Because literacy develops from whole to part, there is no hierarchy of subskills or a logical grade-by-grade sequence (as you learned in Chapter 2, development does follow a clear sequence, and the importance of cognitive subskills is well established in research).

- Literacy develops easily and naturally in response to each child's personal and social needs, and the skills can be learned as easily as spoken language (this false notion has been repeatedly debunked by science; e.g., Dehaene 2009).

- Meaning *always* comes first in language (science shows that word recognition comes first in skilled reading; meaning follows and is an outcome of successful word reading).

- *Never* chop language into bits and pieces to be taught in isolation from whole texts (orthographic learning leading to whole word reading is based upon the sublexical pathway, which is by definition, composed of "bits and pieces"— this is a scientifically shown reality in the establishment of brain words).

In each of these instances, whole language was in fact ignoring the developmental role of the sublexical, sounding out brain pathway to reading. There were, of course, variations of whole language that did include the sublexical pathway with beginners; one notable example is *Kid Writing: A Systematic Approach to Phonics, Journals, and Writing* (Feldgus and Cardonick 1999). But many of the former whole language principles, such as not teaching spelling explicitly, do persist today. Recall that sublexical analysis, sounding words out, and spelling are very much at the heart of orthographic learning—critical for establishing brain words. In many ways whole language was trying to bring about whole word reading without the necessary foundation in place and without regard to how orthographic learning occurs.

Scientists and educators have not been silent in recent years about the whole language movement. Renowned French psychologist Stanislas Dehaene argues convincingly that whole language does "not fit with the architecture of our visual brain" (2009, 195) and goes on to say "Cognitive psychology directly refutes any notion of teaching via a 'global' or 'whole language method'" (2009, 219). Science has spoken!

Phonics and Phonological Awareness

Even though both phonological awareness and phonics were pillars of the National Reading Panel report, science challenges a lot of what we currently do with phonological awareness teaching programs and phonics and how they connect instructionally.

Let's begin with phonological awareness teaching/programs. As acknowledged previously, phonological awareness is a necessary building block to word reading. As such it absolutely needs to be part of the elementary classroom. We now have over forty years of research that clearly shows the developmental progression of phonological awareness skills and how they exert a direct influence on learning to read, and then in turn how learning to read further refines phonological awareness. As outlined by Marilyn Adams in her groundbreaking book, *Beginning to Read: Thinking and Learning About Print* (1990), phonological awareness develops from more basic skills such as rhyming and alliteration to being able to segment words into syllables and blend them back together again, to eventually being able to do the same with individual sounds. Even more advanced phonological awareness continues to develop past first grade as students become able to complete rather sophisticated manipulations of spoken words, including deleting and substituting sounds within words. This more advanced phonological awareness has been directly linked to orthographic learning (e.g., Caravolas, Volín, and Hulme 2005), the mechanism behind the emergence of the Word Form Area and the establishment of brain words.

It needs to be stressed, however, that although phonological awareness is now recognized as a necessary component of reading instruction, it's only part of the equation. Even the most intensive teaching of phonological awareness is not sufficient to bring about the storage of accurate brain words. Furthermore, not all phonological curricula are created equal. Phonological awareness needs to be developmentally sequenced, with practice leading to mastery at each level. And it needs to be taught along with alphabetic knowledge. The two go together. Students need to know the alphabet. They need to know the sounds associated with the letters, and they need to know this at mastery levels to develop fully specified lexical representations (i.e., fully accurate, high-quality brain words). It should be noted that through invented spelling children can explore phonological awareness even as they are learning the alphabet, but to develop efficient word recognition—brain words—students must ultimately master the alphabet. And finally, when it comes to teaching phonological awareness, more is not always better. The returns on phonological awareness teaching reach a ceiling effect at about ten to fifteen minutes per day (Ehri et al. 2001b). Moreover, phonological awareness needs to be incorporated with other efficacious teaching to truly reap its maximum benefit.

KEYPOINT

Even the most intensive teaching of phonological awareness is not enough to bring about the storage of accurate brain words. As described by William Tunmer and colleagues (1988), phonological awareness is "necessary but not sufficient" for learning to read (50).

What about phonics programs? Do they all teach brain words? Let's take a closer look. *Phonics* refers to a method of teaching reading that focuses on mapping letters to sounds and teaching students to decode words by learning the high-frequency combinations including chunking patterns for spelling, single-syllable words, and syllables. Decades of research endorse the efficacy of phonics and have shown that explicit phonics instruction supports learning to read (see the National Reading Panel Report [National Institute of Child Health and Human Development 2000]).

The fact is, however, all phonics approaches and programs are not created equal. The best ones generally incorporate a multisensory approach, but this is not always done. Many teach phonological awareness in isolation instead of as part of a developmentally linked process. Most still fail to connect decoding to sight words, erroneously treating the two routes to reading as completely separate processes.

Furthermore, phonics programs can be overly passive, are too often associated with busywork or worksheets, and may lack the motivational aspects for learning to read. Most do not incorporate a focus on orthographic learning or include spelling as a mechanism to create brain words.

Distinctions between analytic (whole-to-part) and synthetic (part-to-whole phonics often divide phonics advocates and lead to claims that the two approaches are incompatible. There is research to support both approaches, but synthetic phonics does generally receive more support. Yet, analytic phonics can be used to a greater advantage if incorporated in developmental spelling. Having children analyze the sounds within a word in a listening-first approach, and then having them attempt to spell the words, invokes a highly analytical process that can lead the child down the pathway to orthographic learning. Furthermore, spelling actually integrates analytical (in analyzing the sounds) and synthetic (in blending them back together) skills, capturing the best of both worlds. More on this in Chapter 6.

> **TERMINOLOGY TACKLED:**
> ## Analytic Versus Synthetic Phonics
>
> Analytic phonics begins with a whole word and the child analyzes its sounds and letters (whole to parts). Analytic phonics is sometimes associated with the practice of using the first letter to "guess" the word. Synthetic phonics begins with learning the letter-sound parts individually and synthesizing the parts by blending each part into a whole (parts to whole).

In summary, although phonics instruction in general has an impressive research backing, it is far from perfect, especially when it fails to teach brain words.

The Three Cueing System (Including a Caveat for Interpreting Running Records)

A whole language interpretation of the three cueing system is that proficient readers rely on the interdependence between three cueing systems for word identification and comprehension: (1) semantic or meaning cues, (2) syntax or grammar cues, and (3) graphophonic or letter-to-sound cues. Some of the roots of the three cueing system harken back to Marie Clay's early work in New Zealand with primary readers where cueing systems were assessed with running records (Clay 1979) and later to reading miscue analysis (Goodman, Watson, and Burke 1987; Adams 1998). Marie Clay's monumental work called for teachers—especially teachers of beginning reading—to know their students well and keep records of their current reading behavior to see how they progressed over time. Teachers were to observe beginners move through leveled texts, and Clay was confident that well-trained teachers would be able to assess their progress and know when to move them to the next higher level (Clay 1991).

The problem is that many whole language adaptations of this procedure have marginalized phonics or graphophonic cueing within the three cueing system and basically looked at meaning and syntax as driving forces for reading—with phonics and the graphophonic cueing taking on little if any significance (Adams 1998). In common practice, the cues focused on—in order of priority—were meaning (including even guessing from picture cues) and sentence structure, leaving letter-sound associations and the percentage of words recognized correctly at the bottom of the priority list. That's not how the brain's reading circuitry works. Science has shown that successful readers identify words rapidly; the notion that readers primarily cue from context (using meaning and sentence structure) is patently false (Perfetti 2001). And guessing from picture cues is definitely not how efficient readers process text. Retelling a narrative or making a story from a picture walk-through may be useful oral language activities—but this is not how reading skills are acquired, no matter how we may stretch the definition of *reading*. We now know that poor readers, not efficient readers, use contextual cues to guess words (Gough and Juel 1991). Effective readers don't need to guess based on context; rather, they process the text using the graphophonetic cueing system to develop brain words to be able to rapidly read words.

Hundreds of published peer-reviewed research studies have shown that skilled readers are able to rapidly recognize and read printed words, regardless of whether the words are presented in context or in isolation (e.g., Cunningham 2006; Landi et al. 2006; Martin-Chang, Ouellette, and Bond 2017; Wang et al. 2011). When new or difficult words are encountered in context, it is still the letter-sound associations that provide the first and most efficient route to reading, not the meaning or syntax from context.

With this new scientific understanding in mind, perhaps running record priorities should be flipped to highlight how our children are using visual and sound cueing strategies. If a student encounters an unknown word, does he use letter-sound correspondences or syllable chunking based on phonics to decode the word? Does he use graphophonics to self-correct? By focusing on letter-sound associations first or the child's attempt to decode the word, we create an opportunity to match the spelling to the pronunciation to build a brain word for the next time the word is encountered. This is what David Share (2004) describes as "self-teaching," an integral component of orthographic learning that leads to brain words. This opportunity is lost if readers are encouraged to guess the words from context and move on or if synonyms are accepted as "correct" reading. Today, the science of reading calls for more research to investigate ways we can improve the current use of running records and bring this widely used formative assessment more in line with present-day knowledge.

Of course, the importance of word meaning has not been abandoned. We know from science that meaning is anchored to spelling and pronunciation in long-term memory and is an important component of oral language involved in building brain words and proficient reading. Even a partial phonetic decoding can result in an approximated pronunciation that can be matched to oral vocabulary to result in successful reading of the word, thus creating an opportunity to create a brain word (Share 2004). Meaning derived from context can thus indeed help narrow down what the next word may be and can be used to verify the word has been read correctly, but meaning is not the primary cue used by skilled readers to identify words (and research has shown that sentence structure/syntax processing has very little to do with word reading at all [e.g., Vellutino et al. 1996]).

Research in Action

Paying Attention to Word Spelling When Reading

Recently published research by Gene, Sandra Martin-Chang, and Linda Bond (Martin-Chang, Ouellette, and Bond, 2017) directly compared reading accuracy and orthographic learning (i.e., the establishment of brain words) for words read in and out of passage context by second-grade students. After a few exposures, words were read equally well when read within passages or as isolated words. And, in fact, the students showed better orthographic learning—that is, storing new brain words—for the words they had practiced reading outside of the passages/context. This highlights the importance of attending to a word's spelling when reading rather than relying on context cues within a passage; we should not be directing students' attention away from this vital orthographic information when they are reading.

Reading errors where a student substitutes a synonym for the printed word, maintaining meaning while totally ignoring the letters on the page, should not be seen as a preferable type of error to make as is often the case in miscue analysis. Meaning helps verify the correct word choice, but a fully accurate reading creates and accesses brain words with full attention to the word's spelling.

Criticisms of the three-cuing system are far from new. But even today's common practices in classrooms fail to adjust to the science of reading. Twenty years ago prominent reading scholar Marilyn Adams wrote a powerful academic critique of the whole language interpretation of the cueing system, explaining its incompatibility with cognitive science (Adams 1998), as have others more recently (e.g., Primary National Reading Strategy 2006). Yet the whole language view of miscue analysis still unfortunately remains prominent in many of today's classrooms despite incontrovertible evidence of its incompatibility with science.

Inadequate Spelling Instruction: From Haphazard to None at All

Since the advent of whole language, school environments have been apathetic and, at times, hostile to spelling books or programs that teach spelling explicitly and systematically in a grade-by-grade curriculum. It has been three decades since leaders of the whole language movement forcefully and unequivocally called for an end to teaching spelling, arguing: "There should be no special spelling curriculum or regular lesson sequences" (Goodman, Smith, Meredith, and Goodman 1987, 300–301). And, even though this principle has been debunked by today's science, it still persists today, especially among many well-intended administrators who may not know current spell-to-read science or this misguided principle's antiquated whole language genesis. We now know that teaching spelling optimizes reading, including comprehension, by boosting representations in the Word Form Area of the brain where neural representations of spelling are stored and where brain words are developed. Despite this, we continually encounter the following three scientifically unsound instructional practices that are still in use today.

1. No Spelling Instruction. As we travel across the country working with teachers in scores of districts or speaking at conferences, we hear the refrain over and over—"We don't really teach spelling." Test prep has replaced the weekly spelling unit in countless schools with no realization that children would be better readers on the test if we taught them to spell. The argument that "We don't do spelling" is scientifically unsound; reading circuitry is

optimized with automatic word reading for fluency, which greatly benefits from retrieving knowledge of correctly spelled words from the brain's Word Form Area. Compelling new research supports that teaching kids to spell in kindergarten and first grade, using techniques that support the use of invented spelling, not only increases end-of-first-grade reading but also results in better conventional spellers (Ouellette and Sénéchal 2017). And there is now a considerable body of research that shows how spelling instruction brings about improved spelling *and* reading across the elementary school grades (see meta-analysis by Graham and Hebert 2011).

2. Haphazard Spelling Instruction. Haphazard, hit-or-miss spelling instruction is found in scores of schools across North America that have no plan for teaching spelling, no specific grade-by-grade curriculum, or random instruction within a school. In some schools, teachers choose their own words, pulling them from the Internet, while other teachers rarely get around to teaching spelling at all. This results in no continuity or consistency in the spelling curriculum within the school or across the district. Without other options, teachers often turn to the spelling components from their adopted reading

In the Classroom
Disregard for Spelling

Richard hears from hundreds of parents, teachers, and administrators on his educational blog post for *Psychology Today*. Some parents sent the following email response from the principal after they asked why spelling was not being taught: "Spelling is not as much of a focus because of the depth of Common Core Standards that are required to be covered. However, we should still be integrating spelling in the curriculum, such as through writing." These same parents received a similar response from the district supervisor that read: "Using weekly spelling tests for all students does not increase word acquisition or reading comprehension. It does eat up time and give parents something to practice. The Common Core is a rigorous, challenging attempt to move away from things like rote memorization into true understanding of how words work, as well as how language works in context." This response, although well intended, is a holdover of the erroneous whole language theory detailed earlier in this chapter that discredited explicit spelling instruction and derisively labeled systematic spelling instruction as "rote memorization."

Teaching the Right Words at the Right Time

Here's an example of how reading programs often focus on the wrong spelling words. Spelling lessons in first grade should not present too many patterns for the same sound in a single lesson. One popular reading series includes a first-grade spelling weekly unit of study for words with *four* long e spelling patterns. The lesson is entitled "Long e (ea, e, e_e, ee)" and not only includes too many patterns for a single sound in first grade but it also leaves out the common high-frequency consonant-vowel-consonant silent *e* (CVCe, CCVCe) long vowel pattern, which should be taught in first grade. The words in this same lesson range in difficulty from kindergarten level *me* to the very complex homograph *read* (rhyming with *deed*), which could confuse first graders because *read* also can rhyme with *red*. These lessons aren't research based. It's not unusual to find such confusing and developmentally inappropriate lessons in the spelling components of reading programs and kits.

programs, but even these tend to be hit or miss. They may present the wrong words for the grade level and fail to offer a sound grade-by-grade curriculum. Beyond that, the spelling component may compete with other sections or areas of focus bundled within the adoption: vocabulary and oral language, phonological awareness, phonics, sight words, fluency, a text-based comprehension focus, and grammar and writing guidelines and exercises. Remarkably, each of these components likely focuses on different words with no integration, leaving students floundering as spellers.

3. Word Sorting and Hypothesis Testing as a Spelling and Word Study Program. *Word sorting* refers to the practice of having students sort or categorize words based on shared features. For example, words may be sorted into groups based on shared onsets or rimes (e.g., students separate /at/ words spelled *-at* from /in/ words spelled *-in*). In the process students are proposed to be engaged in their own word analysis and hypothesis testing of how words can be grouped together, and they "come up with" the rule or pattern concept. Such activities are common in balanced literacy curricula and commercial programs such as *Words Their Way.*

The positive aspects of word sorting include that it can be motivational if used judiciously and could be included as an instructional activity among several research-based options for teaching spelling. The problem, according to research, is when word sorting is utilized as a *single* strategy system (Sharp, Sinatra, and Reynolds 2008) rather than as part of a *multi*strategy system that interchanges instructional strategies over time and distributes practice in ways that are supported by cognitive psychology (Dunlosky et al. 2013). Many second- through sixth-grade teachers who continue to use word-sorting and hypothesis-testing methods as their primary spelling curriculum—sometimes popular with administrators but often not popular with teachers—may not realize that they are using twenty-year-old whole language methodology that in itself is not a comprehensive, science-based word study program. Nevertheless, this by-product of whole language is still widely used today.

TERMINOLOGY TACKLED:

What Is Balanced Literacy?

Balanced literacy, which is intended to be a balance between phonics and whole language, is difficult to define. We do not critique balanced literacy here because there is no objective criterion for defining this term; programs that call themselves balanced literacy can be implemented differently and may be unrelated to other so-called balanced literacy programs depending on what components of phonics or whole language are chosen in the "balance." For example, would balanced literacy include word sorting alone or would it include other aspects of stand-alone spelling instruction? It could be either way!

Putting It All Together: Toward a Scientifically Based Approach to Reading Instruction

Without spelling knowledge, children are left with incomplete representations of words in memory, which can impede fluent reading and writing. A deep level of spelling knowledge makes words available for lifelong retrieval and application, allowing children to build upon and expand their knowledge. If you can spell it, you can read it. How could anything so simple be so misunderstood? (Gentry 2017a).

In this chapter we considered what the science of reading has to say about current teaching approaches. We showed that while some of these practices do indeed have merit (as do others not specifically reviewed such as guided and shared reading), they are not sufficient alone to bring about the integration of the routes to reading and brain words. And as reviewed here, other long-standing practices really do need to be reconsidered in light of reading science.

The take-home message here is that no teaching approach alone is sufficient and no current programs fully align with what we know about learning to read and the reading brain (for a comprehensive review of specific commercial programs, we recommend the respective chapter in David Kilpatricks' 2015 reading assessment book). There seems to be a missing piece in today's reading instruction—a comprehensive word reading component that integrates phonological awareness, oral language, the routes to reading, and spelling to promote orthographic learning and the creation of brain words. When thinking about current reading and spelling instruction, teaching approaches, and specific programs, we need to ask if they really align with the current scientific study of reading. Do they focus on establishing brain words? And do they do so in ways supported in research and consistent with developmental theory?

In the Classroom

Does Technology Make Spelling Obsolete?

There is an often-cited misguided theory that spelling instruction isn't needed because kids can now use digital tools for spell-checking. "So why," skeptics say, "should we teach spelling at all?" Well, as you have seen, reading circuitry is optimized with automatic word reading for fluency, which greatly benefits from retrieving knowledge of correctly spelled words from the brain's Word Form Area. Those who think we should let computers do the work, rather than our brains, might benefit from this ditty:

Sum won tolled me eye wood knot knead too learn two spell. Computers dew it four us!

Beware of autocorrect!

Too many students struggle in school without an established collection of brain words. By rethinking reading instruction and word study and offering the kind of teaching supported by brain science as well as educational and cognitive psychology, we can greatly improve current educational outcomes and increase the number of students who read well, think well, and write well. We can add the *missing link* to what has been left out of literacy standards and teaching.

KEYPOINT

Questions to Ask of Your Reading Instruction

1. Is it based on a foundation of alphabetic knowledge, phonological awareness, and oral language?

2. Does it integrate alphabetic knowledge, phonological awareness, and phonics knowledge/skills to connect pronunciations to strings of letters in long-term memory?

3. Does it explicitly connect the two routes to reading by linking decoding and sight word reading to build brain words?

4. Does it link listening, spelling, and reading and capitalize on the causal influence of spelling on learning brain words and reading as does our Hear-It, Say-It, Write-It, Read-It, Use-It, spell-to-read approach? (More on this follows in the next chapters.)

5. Is it engaging and developmentally appropriate?

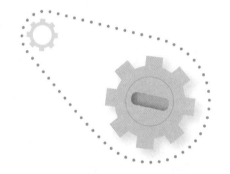

Brain Words: How the Science of Reading Informs Teaching

CHAPTER 5

Phase Observation for Early Spelling to Read

How can you get a quick, accurate, accessible, research-based assessment of an individual's early literacy development that's powerfully supported by cognitive science and neurological research as reported in Chapters 2 and 3 while directly addressing the missing pieces we've discussed in Chapter 4? The answer is *phase observation*.

Early developmental spelling begins with scribbles, transitions to random letters, then to partial alphabetic spellings before moving on to the phase where children make a letter for each sound in a word. Children eventually progress to correctly spelling some words while also using invented spellings containing logical English chunks of phonics patterns. Using phase observation, we can monitor beginning readers' and spellers' progression through five developmental phases and use science-based tools to target instruction to help beginners move forward phase by phase on the pathway to literacy.

Phase observation is literally a window into the child's reading brain. When this basic science—phase observation—becomes part of your regular and ongoing practice, you'll be able to guide your readers in acquiring brain words and establishing the basic reading circuitry necessary that will move

KEYPOINT

In neuroimaging studies with kindergartners, you can essentially see the changes that are happening in readers' brains, and these neurological changes align directly with the shifts in reading and writing that we see during phase observation. One of the advantages of observing the changes in children's early invented spelling is that you can see their concept of how English spelling works changing over time.

them forward through the grades to come. Intervention needs for many struggling readers can be identified much sooner using early phase observation, and targeting instruction with phase observation can help you recognize and guide your students to overcome more serious reading failures, including dyslexia. The longer we wait to intervene, the harder reading failure is to overcome. It makes sense, then, to start in the early phases when we can literally *see* problems developing in our students' spelling abilities.

For over two decades phase observation has received widespread support from research (Ehri 1987, 1997; Ehri and McCormick 2006; Gentry 1977, 1978, 1982, 2000; Gentry and Henderson 1978; Ouellette, Sénéchal, and Haley 2013) and research synthesis (Gentry 2004, 2006; Gentry and Gillette 1993; Moats 2018). In a landmark study titled "Invented Spelling in Kindergarten as a Predictor of Reading and Spelling in Grade 1: A New Pathway to Literacy, or Just the Same Road, Less Known?" Gene and his coauthor Monique Sénéchal (Ouellette and Sénéchal 2017) demonstrated the spelling to read pathway and the importance of developmental changes that occur in young children's spelling. Yet, although phase observation has been used effectively in kindergarten and first-grade classrooms for some time now (e.g., Feldgus and Cardonick 1999; Feldgus, Cardonick, and Gentry 2017) and is supported by the new *PreK–2 Framework for Early Literacy* put forth by the New York City Department of Education (2018), it is not being practiced universally.

In this chapter we'll make it easy for you to "think in phases" as children move from nonreading to reading proficiency by the end of first grade and into second, when the reading brain circuitry has its foundation in place. We'll show you the phases in action and explore how they eloquently demonstrate the interlinking sounding out and orthographic systems of reading introduced in Chapter 2.

Research in Action

Knowledge of Spelling Is the Key

As stated by researcher Marilyn Adams: "The best differentiator between good and poor readers is repeatedly found to be their knowledge of spelling patterns and their proficiency with spelling–sound translations." (Adams 1990, 290)

Literacy Development Reflected in Phase Assessment

In the early phases of developmental spelling, as children stretch through the sounds in each word and try to write each sound they hear letter by letter, writing is a slow and laborious process. This use of invented spelling can help you assess how essential components of reading are coming along; you can see evidence of alphabet knowledge, phonological awareness, phonics, and eventually even capacity for using brain words. That is to say, as children progress you can see a number of words and spelling patterns they've already stored in the Word Form Area of their brains that they can retrieve automatically and spell correctly. Inventing a spelling

Invented spelling, a child's self-generated spelling of a word for which the child has not mastered, is itself an integrated language arts process in the brain.

is itself an integrated language arts process and one that incorporates the critical brain regions of the reading circuit, as identified in Chapter 3. And, as you will see in Chapter 6, a student's invented spelling provides a powerful starting point for targeted reading instruction.

In this chapter we'll show how word reading and developmental spelling are essentially two sides of the same coin. We'll improve your ability to monitor an individual's spelling *and* reading progress, better target instruction, and recognize early on when a child may need intervention and more support. Phase observation is conceivably the *most* powerful first, quick, and accurate reading assessment you can use to get an educated picture of an individual's reading level. Rather than other assessments that require more time and multiple readings at different levels, what you see with your own eyes in a child's invented spelling tells a story of what is happening in her brain at that moment—how she connects the sounds in words to letter and word representations

Phase 0

Phase 1

Phase 2

Phase 3

Phase 4

FIGURE 5.1

Five Phases of Developmental Spelling

in the brain as she puts them down on a page. You see concrete evidence of how the student *thinks* the reading and writing processes work. And, as you'll discover later in this chapter, knowing your students' developmental phases will often direct you to find a range of leveled text they can likely read.

Take a moment to look at the samples of the five phases of children's early writing and spelling shown in Figure 5.1, and you'll notice that it's easy to see a progression of development from one phase to the next. See if you can read each sample.

Notice that you can't possibly read the Phase 0 sample because it doesn't even have alphabetic letters. What you see are letter-like forms.

You might guess the grocery list of three words in Phase 1 starts with *eggs*, but it doesn't say *eggs*; you can't read the list because the letters don't match sounds. The child has merely listed some random letters he can write.

But look at Phase 2. Using the picture as a clue, you can probably read it as *Humpty Dumpty*!

Phase 3 is even more remarkable; you can most likely make out this child's sound-to-letter matches and decode it with ease ("Tooth Fairy. One night I was in my bed and the tooth fairy came."). Although you can read Phase 3, some of the spelling looks odd because every word has one letter for each sound! That's exactly how a Phase 3 speller processes print—both as a word reader when decoding and as a speller when writing.

The problem with the letter-for-each-sound system in Phase 3 is that English doesn't work that way. To break the complex English code and become a proficient reader, children must eventually move to Phase 4 where they've stored a bank of automatically accessible brain words along with logical chunks of phonics patterns that help them recognize syllables to make reading automatic. This reduces the memory load and makes way for comprehension.

Let's look at the Phase 4 sample again in Figure 5.2.

FIGURE 5.2

"My Foot" Phase 4:
Consolidated/Automatic Alphabetic

As you read the Phase 4 sample, think about what this young reader knows about the English language. If you watched him write, you would likely see that he knows many brain words. This end-of-first-grade child wrote: *my, foot, are, feet, take, like, trees, walk, school,* and the like. This is pretty good end-of-first-grade-level spelling. Beyond that, it's easy for you to read the words with the unusual spelling chunks such as *billdings* and *evrewhair* because this child is using the English code, although he doesn't yet have the correct spelling representations in his brain for *buildings* and *everywhere.* Brain words for *buildings* and *everywhere* will be learned in time. What he does know is that the English code is not necessarily *a letter for each sound* (as he was doing in Phase 3). He also shows that he has learned some common spelling patterns. For example, individual letters of phonics patterns such as *a-t* for *at,* as found in *cat, mat, bat, hat,* become *consolidated* into one *at* chunk, allowing new words to be made by simply changing the first letter. With reading and writing practice and self-teaching, these chunks of stored spelling representations in the brain will eventually become sight words or stored chunks of syllable patterns that will be available in later years for decoding many more advanced words such as *catatonic, antimatter, battleship, Manhattan,* and the like.

Remember, Phase 4 is when self-teaching really kicks in. As described in Chapter 2, through experience with print students build and integrate word knowledge, refining the reading circuit in the brain in the process. The end result is self-teaching, orthographic learning, and the creation of brain words. As readers move into and through Phase 4, they are *consolidating* important phonics knowledge such as the CVC short vowel pattern into a word that can be recognized as a chunk. At the same time, this consolidation into chunks is happening with other high-frequency basic first-grade-level phonics patterns and words. With repeated use (the word or chunk being re-presented in the Word Form Area of the brain's mental dictionary and connected to its pronunciation), children first learn to decode the words and then move to a *deeper level of phonics knowledge* so that not only can words be read correctly (decoded), they can be spelled correctly (encoded). With the correctly spelled word representation in the brain, the decodable words become *sight words* automatically connected to meaning—that is to say, they become brain words.

But that's not all! This process also enables the brain to use these sound-to-letter chunks for decoding and encoding syllable patterns, matching them with many more words as the child's language system grows, and eventually these new, more challenging words become automatic sight words once the child has learned the correct spelling, pronunciation, and meaning. So when a child grows up to be a scientist or medical doctor studying _catatonic_ behavior, every time she sees _catatonic_ or writes _catatonic_ that word is re-presented in her brain's Word Form Area; it harkens back the word representation the child put there as a kindergartner or first grader when, as a beginning reader, she went through the early developmental phases of learning to spell and read. Academic, career, and lifelong literacy begins with brain words.

A Closer Look at the Five Phases of Word Reading and Developmental Spelling

In the past researchers have used technical labels such as "selective-cue," "paired-associative," "logographic," "precommunicative," "semiphonetic," and "transitional" to describe the developmental phases readers go through (e.g., Ehri and McCormick 2006; Gentry 2006). Others have incorrectly described developmental phases as "stages" stretching across multiple grade levels and further confused the issue with terms that lack scientific evidence or clarity such as "emergent," "letter name," "within word," "syllables and affixes," and "derivational constancy" (Gentry 2000). We now have the science to give teachers far more evidence-based descriptions of developmental phases.

 Research in Action

Use _Phases_ Not _Stages_

In the current scientific literature, the concept of developmental _phases_ conveys that one phase may gradually move into the next—with adjacent phases possibly overlapping—so that a child may be in Phase 3 moving into Phase 4. _Stages_ conveys a more stringent requirement, often implying a more immediate cutoff from one period of development to the next, as if climbing a staircase where you can be on only one step at a time (Ehri and McCormick 2006). We now know development is more accurately depicted as _phases_ rather than as absolute _stages_.

The current literature makes thinking in phases teacher-friendly, and we do so here by using consistent terminology for both the Ehri word reading phases and Gentry's spelling phases, which dovetail very closely even though they were discovered in two independent lines of research (Ehri 1987; Gentry 1982, 2006; New York City Department of Education 2018). To keep things clear and teacher-friendly, we've simplified the labeling from current and past research into five clear, meaningful phase labels to help you work with them more easily and more effectively. Let's look at each of our samples one last time in Figures 5.3 through 5.6 to make it easier for you to "think in phases."

FIGURE 5.3
Phase 0:
Non-Alphabetic

Phase 0 word readers and writers are unable to use the alphabet. Phase 0 spellers may use approximations of letters, but they don't know the letters of the alphabet, so as you can see in Figure 5.3 there are no letters. In attempting to read words in Phase 0, the child does not use the letters in the word to cue reading because she has no alphabetic knowledge. The child may recognize a few words from memory when she sees them in the environment. For example, the child may recognize *Pepsi* because she remembers it on the can but won't be able to read *Pepsi* if encountered in print elsewhere.

FIGURE 5.4
Phase 1:
Pre-Alphabetic

This grocery list says *milk, Raisin Bran,* and *doughnuts.* Pre-alphabetic spellers use letters, but they do not know that the letters represent the sounds of the word they are attempting to write. Generally, they have very limited letter knowledge; for example, in the sample in Figure 5.4 you see *e*'s, *o*'s, and *s*'s repeated in each word. The letters appear to be random. With Phase 1 pre-alphabetic word readers, the letters are basically ignored. Phase 1 readers aren't using letters to read words because they do not understand that letters represent sounds in the spoken word. They can't decode, and just as in Phase 0, if they see *Pepsi* anywhere except on the can or bottle, they can't read it. For both spelling and writing they use nonphonetic visual or environmental cues such as the Pepsi can, which of course are arbitrary cues. Phase 1, the pre-alphabetic phase, comes *before* children can use an alphabetic system to match letters to sounds or sounds to letters, thus we call it *pre-alphabetic*. It's *before* they begin using the alphabet letters in an alphabetic system to help them.

FIGURE 5.5

Phase 2:
Partial Alphabetic

Phase 2 writers and readers make a giant cognitive leap. They are beginning to see how the alphabetic system works! You will see them start *using* the alphabet to spell and even to read words by matching *some* of the letters to sounds in their spoken language albeit their knowledge of the system is limited. You will see Phase 2 letter-sound spelling mappings that look abbreviated just like *HMT DPD* for *Humpty Dumpty* in Figure 5.5. The word reading is likewise limited to cueing on only some of the letters. Because processing spelling and word reading in this phase involves only *part* of the letters in words for both spelling and reading, Phase 2 is called partial alphabetic. Children in Phase 2 are unable to use full phonemic segmentation ability with letter matches for either spelling or reading words. These students need to further refine their phonological awareness and need more focused and engaged experience with print to continue their progress down the pathway to literacy.

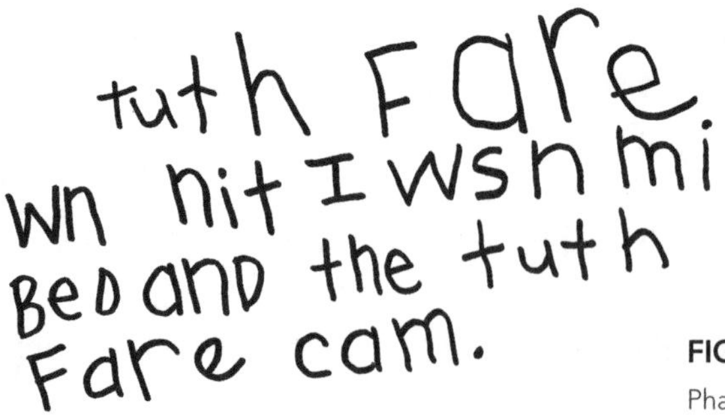

tuth Fare.
wn nit I wsh mi
Bed and the tuth
Fare cam.

FIGURE 5.6

Phase 3:
Full Alphabetic

Phase 3 spelling in most cases is "a letter for a sound" spelling. With full alphabetic spelling virtually every sound in the word is represented, but the spelling is slow and deliberate. Often you can hear a child say the sound and then watch as he writes the letter for that sound in the word. Almost all of the sounds are represented in each word in the Phase 3 sample in Figure 5.6. For example, you can see how the child spelled *nit* for (/n/ /ī/ /t/) in *night* and *cam* for (/k/ /ā/ /m/) in *came*. Common one-letter-for-a-sound spellings in Phase 3 include letter name spelling for long vowels in the CVCe pattern (*tip* for *type*; *mak* for *make*); sound spellings such as *ate* for *eighty*; one-letter spellings for vowel digraphs (i.e., *ai, ea, ay, ee, ow*) as in *pla* for *play* and *kep* for *keep*; sound spellings for inflectional endings (*ratz* for *rats*; *smakt* for *smacked*), and incorrect sound spellings for short vowels (*bet* for *bit*; *hit* for *hot*).

There are a few special sound features for which Phase 3 spellers represent *two* sounds with one letter, which are exceptions to the one-letter-for-a-sound strategy. It's important to note these few exceptions because they are prominent in Phase 3 writing and very helpful in identifying Phase 3 spellers. The exceptions to the one-letter-for-a-sound strategy include the following:

- Syllabic *r*'s carry the vowel sound in *r*-controlled vowels in spellings such as *brd* for *bird* or *prd* for *purred*.

- Syllabic sonorants allow *l* and *m* to carry the vowel sound in spellings such as *tabl* for *table* and *posm* for *possum*.

- In preconsonantal nasals (where *n* or *m* precedes a consonant), Phase 3 spellers systematically leave out the *m* or *n*, rendering spellings such as *stap* for *stamp* and *bop* or *bup* for *bump*.

Note that the word *monster* (which you will use for assessment in the Monster Test) includes both a preconsonantal nasal *and* a syllabic *r*. Phase 3 spellers systematically spell this word *mostr*, which in fact represents all of its sounds: *m* for the /m/, *o* for the /ŏ/, *s* before a consonant for /ns/, and *r* for the /ər/ sound because the *r* carries the vowel sound (Gentry 2006; Read 1986).

In Phase 3 full alphabetic word reading—cueing on a letter for each sound—greatly increases the volume of words children can read. For example, similarly spelled words such as *king* and *kick* can be read and *pink* might even help the child figure out *ink*. Here we see the routes to reading begin to come together as sound and word knowledge is gained. Children in this phase are generally successful with sound-by-sound, letter-by-letter processing, but a word like *interesting* with its eleven graphophonic (letter-to-sound) units presents a challenge: i n t (ə) r ə s t i n g. Try sounding out that one letter by letter! The full alphabetic phase precedes chunking where *interesting* becomes *in-tur-est-ing* for spelling and is likewise sounded out in chunks as *in-ter-est-ing* for word reading (Ehri and McCormick 2006).

We inspected the chunking characteristics of Phase 4, the consolidated/automatic alphabetic phase, in the "My Foot" story in Figure 5.2. It's important to remember that Phase 4 really jump-starts the express pathway in the Word Form Area, using consolidated chunks of phonics patterns for automatic recognition as children map to other words, including polysyllabic words for quicker and easier decoding. Here, for example, words such as *pancake* and *catnip* are more easily decoded. In Phase 4, the routes to reading truly intersect and the internal store of brain words expands through self-teaching and orthographic learning as detailed in Chapters 2 and 3. The focus in this phase is on decoding and encoding whole words or chunks as children use brain words and larger units of phonics patterns that recur in different words for both reading and spelling (Ehri 1991; Ehri and McCormick 2006; Frith 1985; Gentry 1982). These Phase 4 chunks include prefixes, suffixes, root words, onset patterns, rime patterns, and syllable patterns drawing largely from Anglo-Saxon derivations but even occasionally from Latin and Greek (Moats 2015/2016; Henry 1989). Phase 4 is a very big deal because it is when independent reading, self-teaching, orthographic learning, and the express pathway to more efficient spelling and reading kick in.

Easy Early Assessment with the Monster Test
(The Gentry Developmental Spelling Test)

Gentry's Monster Test of developmental spelling (1985), newly supported by what we know from cognitive psychology and neuroscience, has been in use for over thirty years. It's a ten-item test with words selected based on research-derived sound features that children spell in different ways at different phases of development.

 Research in Action

Research-Based Sound Features Found in the Monster Test

The sounds featured in the Monster Test words include long and short vowels (*eighty, dress*), preconsonantal nasals (*stamp*), syllabic sonorants (*dragon*), *-ed* endings (*hiked*), retroflex vowels (*purred*), affricates (*truck*), and intervocalic flaps (*bottom*) (Gentry 1978; Gentry and Henderson 1978; Read 1970, 1975).

The test is a quick way to determine your students' developmental phases and is an effective way to show progress over time. It can be administered up to four times a year to detect progress or lack of progress, and it can also help you place your students into appropriate ranges of leveled texts so you can target instruction that's developmentally appropriate (Feldgus, Cardonick, and Gentry 2017). For example, you can easily determine if your students have mastered essential first-grade-level short vowel patterns and inflectional endings with the Monster Test.

The Monster Test is built on the expectation that children progress over time through the five developmental phases in order as discussed earlier. If a child is not moving through the phases appropriately across time, this could be a symptom of learning disability and possibly an early indication of the need for dyslexia screening and early intervention.

The spelling list for the Monster Test and its sentences are shown in Figure 5.7. Note that this is different from a traditional spelling test, because kids aren't expected to practice or prepare for it and you aren't looking for perfect spelling. Rather, you want your students to use their invented spelling on unfamiliar words to see what they know about the spelling process. For instance, you'll probably notice that these fairly advanced words aren't words we'd generally expect kindergarten and first graders

FIGURE 5.7

Monster Test Word List

1.	monster	The boy was eaten by a **MONSTER**.
2.	united	You live in the **UNITED** States.
3.	dress	The girl wore a new **DRESS**.
4.	bottom	A big fish lives at the **BOTTOM** of the lake.
5.	hiked	We **HIKED** to the top of the mountain.
6.	human	Miss Piggy is not a **HUMAN**.
7.	eagle	An **EAGLE** is a powerful bird.
8.	closed	The little girl **CLOSED** the door.
9.	bumped	The car **BUMPED** into the bus.
10.	type	**TYPE** the letter on the computer keyboard.

Monster Test Word List. Updated and Adapted from Gentry (1985–2018).

to spell correctly. Again, that's not the goal. You want to see how your children are processing the words in their brains so you can determine their phase. When most of the words are spelled correctly, children have moved out of the developmental phases and typically into second-grade spelling and reading levels or higher.

Administering the Monster Test (Updated and Adapted from Gentry 1985–2018)

The Monster Test was designed for pupils in kindergarten through first grade and for second-grade struggling readers, but it can be administered to students at upper levels as well. Simply call out each word in the spelling list, give the sentence provided, and call out the word again without giving any prompts beyond that. Because you want to see how your students invent the spelling, you might say, "Spell the sounds that you hear." Explain that the activity will not be graded as right or wrong, but that it will be used to see how the student "thinks" certain "very hard words" should be spelled. Be encouraging and make the activity challenging and fun. Tell younger students that they are doing "big kid spelling" with words like the ones that older students get in school.

After you administer the ten-word spelling list, group each of the responses into one of the five developmental phases with a score that correlates to its phase (0 for Phase 0, 1 for Phase 1, 2 for Phase 2, and so on). If the word is spelled correctly, give it a check mark. You will not be getting a sum of these scores; rather, use these score designations to count the number of responses that fall into each of the phases, so you can see which phase comes up the most. Figure 5.8 is an example of a scored Monster Test. More detail on analyzing the spellings is provided on the following pages.

How to Analyze the Spellings

Before going further, think once more about the features that you will look for in each word to place it in a developmental phase. Note that for veteran teachers who may have previously used more technical spelling labels (e.g., precommunicative—transitional), we include those former labels in the following list to remind you that the phases simply have been renamed to make them more teacher-friendly. Here, we'll revisit the phases of spelling as we reflect specifically on responses to the Monster Test and include the grade-level expectation for each spelling phase. As a final note, remember that a child who scribbles and cannot write his name is in Phase 0 (non-alphabetic), which is generally expected in preschool.

FIGURE 5.8

Analysis

	Word	Spelling	Phase	Explanation
1.	monster	*mostr*	3	Though Phase 3 usually includes a letter for each sound, here the omission of preconsonantal *n*, along with syllabic *r*, makes *mostr* a Phase 3 spelling (see our previous discussion of Phase 3 indicators).
2.	united	*unitd*	3	A letter used for each sound.
3.	dress	*jrs*	2	Partial phonetic because vowel sound is omitted.
4.	bottom	*botm*	3	All sounds represented by one letter; sonorant *m* carries the vowel sound.
5.	hiked	*hik*	2	Final sound omitted making it partial.
6.	human	*humon*	4	Spelled in two consolidated chunks (*hu-mon*).
7.	eagle	*egl*	3	Each sound is represented.
8.	closed	*closd*	3	All sounds represented by one letter.
9.	bumped	*bmt*	2	Left out some sounds.
10.	type	*tip*	3	All sounds represented by one letter.

Analysis: There are three Phase 2 spellings, six Phase 3 spellings, and one Phase 4 spelling.
Because the majority of the responses fall into Phase 3, the results indicate that the child is in Phase 3.

Phase 1 Pre-Alphabetic Spelling (formerly precommunicative spelling): Expected no later than the first half of kindergarten. This is the "babbling" stage of spelling. Children use letters for writing words, but the letters are strung together randomly and you can't read them. The letters in Phase 1 spelling do not correspond to sounds. Examples: *opsps* = *eagle*; *rtat* = *eighty*.

"If-Then" Developmental Scoring: If the spelling looks like random letters with no sound-to-letter matches, it's Phase 1.

Phase 2 Partial Alphabetic Spelling (formerly semiphonetic spelling): Expected no later than the end of kindergarten. This is when spellers first know that letters represent sounds. They perceive and represent reliable sounds with partial sound-letter spellings. Spellings are often abbreviated, representing initial and/or final sounds. Examples: *eg* = eagle; *at* = *eighty*.

"If-Then" Developmental Scoring: If the spelling has any letters that map to the sounds in the word but is not a full mapping as in Phase 3, it's Phase 2. *E* by itself or *eg* are examples of Phase 2 spellings for *eagle*. *M* or *mst* or *mstr* are Phase 2 spellings for *monster*.

Phase 3 Full Alphabetic Spelling (formerly phonetic spelling): Expected no later than the middle of first grade. Students in this phase almost always spell words with a letter for each sound. They perceive and represent all of the phonemes in a word, though spellings may be unconventional. Children in Phase 3 often use a technique called finger spelling to determine the sounds in a word, and they write a letter for each sound. Try finger spelling each Monster Test word yourself: beginning with the thumb followed by the pointer finger and then the next finger and so forth, say each sound, and as you say it use one letter to write that sound. You should get spellings such as *egl* for *eagle* (three phonemes), *botm* for *bottom*, *unitd* for *united*, and even *ate* for *eighty*. As mentioned earlier, there are a few exceptions to the one-letter-for-each-sound strategy in cases where one letter can represent two sounds such as syllabic *r*'s as in *brd* for *bird* and *prd* for *purred* and sonorant *n*'s and *l*'s as in *chekn* for *chicken* and *litl* for *little*.

"If-Then" Developmental Scoring: If the spelling includes one letter for each sound or one letter that carries two sounds, then the spelling is Phase 3.

Phase 4 Consolidated/Automatic Alphabetic Spelling (formerly transitional spelling): Expected by the end of first grade. Children in Phase 4 spell words in chunks of letter patterns using their knowledge of phonics patterns. They may think about how words appear visually; a visual memory of spelling patterns is apparent. Spellings exhibit conventions of English orthography like vowels in every syllable, VCe and vowel digraph patterns, correctly spelled inflectional endings, and memory of recurring English letter sequences in chunks of phonics patterns. Examples: *egil* for *eagle*; *eightee* for *eighty*; *jumpped* for *jumped*.

"If-Then" Developmental Scoring: If the invented spelling has a vowel in every syllable, *-ed* and *-ing* spelled correctly, short vowels spelled correctly, and looks like a logical English spelling, it's Phase 4. Logical English spelling patterns include some vowel team spellings in Phase 4. You'll see spellings such as *eagul, bottum, hicked, tipe, monstur*, and even *younighted*.

Conventional Spelling (formerly correct spelling): Expected throughout elementary and high school. Children develop brain words over years of systematic explicit spelling study while expanding their vocabulary and spoken language system through reading and writing. In this phase, correct spelling is categorized by instructional grade-level expectations. For example, spelling a majority of words that can be spelled by the average fourth grader would indicate fourth-grade-level conventional spelling. Place the word in this category if it is spelled correctly and score it with a check mark.

"If-Then" Developmental Scoring: If the spelling is correct, use a ✓ to indicate it is conventional.

Scoring the Monster Test

Once you have an understanding of the expectations within each developmental phase, scoring the students' spellings becomes much more straightforward; in our experience, teachers tend to become familiar with the scoring process rather quickly. A scoring chart is provided in Figure 5.9 that can help you analyze the spelling, in conjunction with the following guidelines:

1. Look at the student's spelling for each word. Score it as 0, 1, 2, 3, 4, or use a check mark if the word is spelled correctly. Note that 0 is non-alphabetic; its not really a spelling—it's scribbling or letter-like forms. Note that a check mark is correct conventional spelling. If you aren't sure, find the error type in the chart provided in Figure 5.9.

2. Indicate the appropriate developmental label—Phase 0, Phase 1, Phase 2, Phase 3, Phase 4, or ✓—next to the word on the student's spelling list by simply writing the phase number (0, 1, 2, 3, 4, or ✓) matching the developmental spelling phase beside each of the ten spelling words.

3. Determine how many of the ten words fall into each phase category. For example, there may be three Phase 2 words and seven Phase 3 words.

4. If half or more of the student's spellings are in a particular phase, that's the child's phase level. If a majority of the spellings are conventionally correct (scored as ✓), the child has likely moved out of the early developmental phases into second-grade levels or above. Sometimes children are mostly in one phase but moving into the next phase. Even though ten words is a small sample, this test will reveal the types of developmental errors that a student is likely to make in free writing. If you see a conglomeration of mixed phases, that's a red flag indicating that the child might not be progressing typically and may need careful monitoring or intervention.

FIGURE 5.9

Monster Test Word List

Word		Phase 1 Pre-Alphabetic Spelling	Phase 2 Partial Alphabetic Spelling	Phase 3 Full Alphabetic Spelling	Phase 4 Consolidated/Automatic Alphabetic Spelling	Conventional
1.	monster	Random Letters	mtr	mostr	monstur	monster
2.	united	Random Letters	u	unitd	younighted	united
3.	dress	Random Letters	jrs	jras	dres	dress
4.	bottom	Random Letters	bt	bodm	bottum	bottom
5.	hiked	Random Letters	h	hikt	hicked	hiked
6.	human	Random Letters	um	humn	humun	human
7.	eagle	Random Letters	el	egl	egul	eagle
8.	closed	Random Letters	kd	klosd	clossed	closed
9.	bumped	Random Letters	b	bopt	bumpped	bumped
10.	type	Random Letters	tp	tip	tipe	type

Updated and Adapted from Gentry (1985–2018).

Monitor Phase Development in Children's Everyday Writing

In addition to monitoring progress with the Monster Test, we suggest you verify your results by observing your students' invented spellings in their first-draft writing samples. Using your knowledge of the developmental phases and the Monster Test scoring system, you can easily become an expert at identifying your students' phase levels, which allows you not only to decipher their invented spellings but also to recognize what these approximations tell you about their development. This is known as a "close look writing assessment" (Feldgus, Cardonick, and Gentry 2017). Note that when you use spellings from a child's writing, it is generally necessary to look at enough writing to find at least five to ten invented spellings to get a good sample. Keep in mind that students who are at lower developmental levels may have memorized spellings for some words such as *c-a-t, cat*. It is their misspellings, however, that provide "windows into their minds" to reveal their developmental level of spelling, word reading, and writing and help you monitor their progress.

Read the "Earth Quakes" story in Figure 5.10 written by a kindergartner near the end of the year. When you have finished reading it, we will list each invented spelling and do a close look writing assessment (adapted from Feldgus, Cardonick, and Gentry 2017, used with permission).

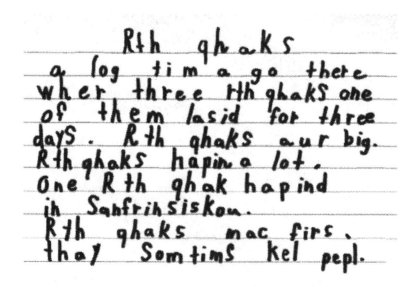

FIGURE 5.10

Kindergartner's "Earth Quakes" Story

We are able to analyze each invented spelling to get a measure of what phase this kindergartner is in even from this small sample. In Figure 5.11, we list and analyze each of his approximations using this guide:

- Each invented spelling is marked as Phase 3 if it has a letter for each sound.
- Each invented spelling is marked as Phase 4 if it has logical phonics patterns consolidated into chunks. (Note that there are no Phase 0–2 spellings in the "Earth Quakes" sample.).

FIGURE 5.11

Phase Analysis of the "Earth Quakes" Story— A Close Look Writing Assessment

	Invented Spelling	Phase	Phase Strategy
1.	*Rth* (earth)	3	*r* for the *r*-controlled vowel; he knows the digraph *th*
2.	*qhaks* (quakes)	3	*qh* for /kw/, *a* for /ā/, *k* for /k/, and *s* for /s/
3.	*log* (long)	3	*l* for /l/, *o* for /ä/, and typical omission of a preconsonantal nasal before *g*
4.	*tim* (time)	3	*t* for /t/, *i* for /ī/, and *m* for /m/
5.	*mac* (make)	3	*m* for /m/, *a* for /ā/, and *k* for /k/
6.	*kel* (kill)	3	*k* for /k/, *e* for /ĭ/, *l* for /l/
7.	*pepl* (people)	3	*p* for /p/, *e* for /ē/, *p* for /p/, and *l* for /l/
8.	*Sanfrinsiskou* (San Francisco)	4	syllable chunks for *san-frin-sis-kou*
9.	*hapin* (happen)	4	Syllable chunks for *hap-in*

There is a lot to celebrate in this child's close look writing analysis! What immediately jumps out is that he is advanced for kindergarten and making progress toward becoming a proficient reader. He is likely moving from Phase 3 into Phase 4 as both a writer and a reader. While celebrating his meaning making and other strengths, this sample helps us target instruction for CVC short vowels, the long vowel CVCe pattern, digraphs *qu* and *ng*, and eventually *r*-controlled syllables as well as the idea that every syllable needs a vowel. Taking a close look at students' first-draft writing samples is another way phase observation can be a powerful everyday tool for assessment, monitoring progress, and planning both individual and group instruction.

Where to Go from Here

Phase observation is a boon to early literacy success for spellers, readers, and writers and a powerful tool for reading teachers. Making the connection between spelling and reading is a transformational concept and a missing link that can lead to better reading and higher test scores. The developmental phases of spelling and word reading discussed in this chapter have considerable potential to help us wield science-based tools to match research-based techniques with each child's developmental level. With phase observation as a universal starting point, we can offer appropriate instruction and teacher scaffolding for individuals at the right time and teach children to spell, read, and write.

In the remaining chapters, we present our spell-to-read teaching method that starts with a child's invented spelling and explicitly teaches word reading by helping students develop brain words (Chapter 6); phase assessment provides guidance on the starting point and allows you to monitor your students' progress, development, and response to instruction. We then conclude our discussion with a look at students beyond first grade (Chapter 7) and students with dyslexia (Chapter 8).

In the Classroom

Phase Observation and Text Levels

Although a full exploration of phase observation and targeted instruction is beyond the scope of this book, it is helpful to highlight the alignment between the developmental phases discussed here and the various ranges of leveled text used in many kindergarten and first-grade classrooms. This is summarized in the following table:

Phase	Text Demands/Responses	Text Levels	Examples	
0	Responding to read-alouds with repeated reading and dialogue reading. Memory reading of words and phrases and a few favorite books such as Dr. Seuss's *The Foot Book* but no decoding.	Read-alouds; picture books	*The Foot Book* by Dr. Seuss and texts such as *Mrs. Wishy-Washy and the Big Wash*	
1	Memory reading and gradual release of level A easy books such as *The Pancake*. No independent decoding evident yet.	Fountas & Pinnell level A Lexile level: BR-70	*The Pancake* by Roderick Hunt and Alex Brychta and other leveled texts such as *Butterfly*	
2	Memory reading and gradual release of level A–C easy books such as *The Cat on the Mat*. Some use of letter-to-sound associations indicating initial signs of decoding. Recognition of a few sight words.	Fountas & Pinnell levels A–C Lexile level: BR-70	*Cat on the Mat* by Brian Wildsmith and other leveled texts such as *Wishy-Washy Ice Cream*	
3	Memory reading and gradual release of level C–G easy books such as *Zoo-Looking*. Ability to decode many more words. More words recognized automatically.	Fountas & Pinnell levels C–G Lexile level: 80–450	*Zoo-Looking* by Mem Fox and other leveled texts such as *The Boy and the Gumballs*	
4	Independent reading of levels G–I easy chapter books such as *Little Bear*. Moving into independent reading. Self-teaching becomes evident. Great increase in recognition of phonics patterns and automatic recognition of brain words.	Fountas & Pinnell levels H–J Lexile level: 451–550	*Little Bear* by Elsa Holmelund Minarik and Maurice Sendak and other leveled texts such as *The Heron and the Swan*	

CHAPTER 6

Spell-to-Read: Building Brain Words in Kindergarten and First Grade

Throughout this book we've endeavored to present a systematic and accessible synopsis of leading developmental theory, behavoral research, and current knowledge of the reading brain in an effort to support you as you evaluate approaches to literacy instruction and implement practices in the classroom that are truly scientifically based. Now, with the power of phase assessment in mind, we will consider the *how* of reading instruction and word study. Here, we present an overview of how you can put all of this research and knowledge about the developing brain to work in teaching word reading. In this chapter we outline our spell-to-read approach to reading instruction, which capitalizes on the science of reading to help you build ever-so-important brain words for your beginning readers.

Recall the conclusions from the scientific study of reading we presented at the end of Chapter 3.

1. Word reading is built upon a foundation of speech and oral language and is an essential teaching outcome.

2. Word reading requires decoding, and decoding requires the integration of alphabetic knowledge, phonological awareness, and phonics knowledge/ skills to connect pronunciations to strings of letters in long-term memory.

3. The routes to reading intersect in development: efficient word reading requires an explicit connection between decoding and sight word reading as the Word Form Area emerges in the developing brain.

4. Brain words are established through orthographic learning as the routes to reading intersect.

5. Listening, speaking, spelling, and reading share brain processes and stored representations. Listening and spelling activities directly integrate the reading routes and associated brain regions and lead directly to the development of brain words.

6. The development of a fully functioning, highly integrated reading circuit can be facilitated by aligning our teaching with what we now know about developmental theory and brain-imaging research.

With all this in mind, we propose a spell-to-read approach to teaching reading that incorporates each of these conclusions. This evidence-based technique for teaching beginning readers goes above and beyond typical word study. Why? Because unlike other approaches, it integrates the foundational skills of reading and develops the intertwined routes to reading—through listening and spelling. The research we presented in previous chapters confirms that spelling instruction is often the missing piece for early literacy. Spelling presents us with a powerful way to create accurate, high-quality stored spelling and word representations—aka brain words—that ignite the reading brain and open the door to continued literacy success. In this approach, deep-level word analysis replaces simple ineffective, passive exposure such as word wall exercises or other, less effective, rote memorization routines. The spell-to-read method leads students to better understandings because it's matched directly to their growing phases of development. Building this essential reading dictionary in the brain while deepening their word analysis skills puts young readers firmly on the pathway to literacy.

Spell-to-Read: A Listening-First Approach

In place of unrelated, disconnected lessons, a spell-to-read approach integrates work on phonological awareness, decoding (phonics), encoding (spelling), and visual (sight) word recognition so that children end up with a correct spelling representation in their brains—and it's not just memorization. Most traditional approaches such as "Look-Say," rote memory of flash cards, word sorts, and even "phonics-first" begin with visual exposure to the word or to a letter. In contrast, a spell-to-read approach begins with phonological awareness and an auditory analysis of the sound structures. Based on this analysis, students generate their first invented spellings, and the teacher then scaffolds and guides students toward the correct spelling—using those initial spelling attempts as a starting point. Along the way, targeted instruction further refines students' decoding and word recognition skills. The outcome: brain words for continued literacy success.

In this approach, the typical sequencing of teaching reading is flipped on its head. In brief, instead of exposing students to print and expecting them to magically become readers, a word is first presented aurally and students are asked to analyze its sounds. Then, students are encouraged to spell the word as they heard it. This process both activates and promotes auditory processing and phonological awareness while engaging students in a deep, self-directed analytical process. In doing so, they activate brain regions known to be critical for language and reading, integrating them in the process. The sound-processing centers in the brain lay the groundwork for visual processing (at the back of the brain) to connect with speech sound planning and production (at the front of the brain). In essence, the brain's reading circuitry lights up, increasing processing and engagement while starting the word down the pathway to becoming a permanent part of the student's collection of brain words. The student's spelling is eventually contrasted with the correct spelling and from that point on, as the word is used in reading and writing activities, it further integrates the reading pathways, establishing lasting syllable and word representations that are stored in a child's memory for future reading and spelling use. Through this process, brain words are created—not through ineffective osmosis or memorization—but through interactive, integrative processing based on developmental theory and brain research.

 ## Research in Action

A rose is a ROSE is a rOsE

One fascinating reality of reading is that we can read words regardless of how they may be presented visually—different fonts, handwriting styles, and so on. Sure, we have all had that professor or family doctor whose handwriting we just couldn't decipher, but research has shown that for the most part, we can deal with a tremendous degree of variability in the appearance of print. This is because our brain words are not visual pictures per se but abstract neuronal (brain) representations, which are coded in a complex electrical and chemical signal. We recognize sequences of letters regardless of appearance because in our brains they are stored as connected to—or anchored in memory by—the sounds or pronunciations they match. It is through listening and auditory analysis that word spellings—our brain words—can start becoming anchored in memory via the process of orthographic learning or mapping, as described in Chapter 2.

This listening-first, spell-to-read approach to teaching reading is essentially an integrated, evidence-based type of word study that can be added to any current approach or program being followed in the classroom. It can be used for whole-class instruction and is just as suitable for remedial small-group or individual instruction. It is versatile and effective and can actually save you valuable time in addressing a multitude of developmental skills in one, engaging activity. Over the following pages we will show you how this can be done as structured word study lessons, integrated with other literacy teaching, and/or applied in the moment in a literacy-rich classroom.

The spell-to-read lesson sequence is fairly straightforward and easy to implement in any classroom. Just remember, it is a listening-first approach in which the student will initially engage their auditory processing and make connections between what they hear and their knowledge of print. We want to integrate phonological awareness with our reading instruction, so we can support students as they create brain words. This can all be done seamlessly by following our engaging *five-step sequence* for students (don't worry, more detail is provided on each step in the pages to come):

Step 1 **Hear-It.** Always start with a listening activity—no print! It is best to start with an auditory phonological awareness activity, which involves auditory analysis and phonological working memory. In this step, make sure the target words are understood—remember, vocabulary meaning is important to building brain words as well.

Step 2 **Say-It.** Students need to have the opportunity to articulate the word's pronunciation. This involves speech production and introduces self-directed word analysis; students are taught to stretch through the word to begin the process of analyzing the sounds within words.

Step 3 **Write-It.** In this step, students write the word and its sounds—as they heard it. Note, you have not shown them the actual printed word yet. This internal word analysis before actually seeing the word leads students to convert what they hear into a child-generated spelling attempt. After that, guide them through the correct spelling to help them build an accurate brain-based representation. There are many ways this can be done, and we will explore these shortly.

Step 4   **Read-It.** Now the students read a correct model of the word just taught. This activates their reading brains with both decoding and sight word reading opportunities as students apply phonics knowledge in decoding and build brain words for future encounters with the word in the process. This is where self-teaching can kick in and the routes to reading become intertwined.

Step 5   **Use-It.** Once the words have been taught, use them in a host of literacy activities and approaches already present in your classroom. As children develop the reading circuits in their brains, they master words and more efficient, rapid word recognition is achieved—for all word types.

Structured Weekly Word Study Lessons Following the Spell-to-Read Approach

We recommend explicit word study lessons for each day of the week following our listening-first, spell-to-read approach that can be accomplished in as little as ten to fifteen minutes a day. These daily activities build brain words through the word study component of your language arts block. Once everyone is comfortable with the procedures, these activities are repeated in subsequent weeks to teach a new block of words each week. Use your school's or district's traditional spelling list if you have one, but if not, don't worry. We will provide guidelines for word selection and tips for dividing words into weekly units or blocks shortly. You may choose to focus on just a few words each day or increase the number of words depending on your students' needs and the time you wish to spend on these activities daily. Your brain word lessons can be accomplished in as little as fifteen minutes a day.

> **KEYPOINT**
>
> Our spell-to-read, listening-first *five-step sequence*—Hear-It, Say-It, Write-It, Read-It, Use-It—can easily be incorporated into any classroom and builds a dictionary of key words in each beginning reader's brain that will be available for a lifetime of use.

Once you are armed with your weekly block of words, you can plan your activities around our five-step sequence (Hear-It, Say-It, Write-It, Read-It, Use-It). On the first day of the week, we recommend focusing solely on listening and speaking (Hear-It and Say-It), but for the remainder of the week we plan to target all five of our steps in each lesson (i.e., all steps are included in each subsequent day of the week). As you explore the following sample week-long plan, notice how the five-step sequence manifests over a typical week.

Day 1

On the first day of the week the goal is auditory bombardment and familiarization of all of the week's words. These terms mean exactly what you might infer. We *bombard* or flood the students with sound to tune up the hearing and sound-processing brain areas known to be involved in the neurological reading circuit. As students become familiar with the sounds of these words, through repeatedly hearing and saying them, we start to integrate speech and hearing processing. This is also the time to ensure they understand what the words mean so that we're linking sound and meaning in their brains. This initial process helps set the stage for phonological awareness and processing. Traditional phonological awareness tasks are done using the week's words. Let's consider what a typical Hear-It and Say-It Day 1 would look like, activity by activity.

In the Classroom

Stretching Through the Sounds

Stretching through the sounds is a technique in which a word is pronounced in a slow-motion fashion and its individual sounds are stretched (where possible). The word is still pronounced as a unit—there is no pausing between the sounds. Teachers can draw a student's attention to particular parts of the word by simply saying those sounds louder and/or with increased stress. This is sometimes called "stretching through the sounds with a moving target."

A. The teacher introduces the week's words by saying each word repeatedly, both at a normal rate and slowly, stretching through the sounds. This is the start of the auditory bombardment and familiarization and will always be the first step of instruction (Hear-It).

B. The teacher discusses word meaning and verifies student comprehension. You can use the words in sentences and ask students to create sentences too. Remember there is no print involved yet—this is all done orally. Opposites and synonyms can be discussed as appropriate, and if you find it helpful, you can show pictures of the words.

C. The students are given opportunity to articulate the words, both at a normal pace and by stretching through the sounds. Hand spelling can be introduced to link speech production with sound-segmenting awareness.

Step 1:
Say the word
(fist)

Step 2:
Thumb up for
onset.

Step 3:
Handshake
for rime.

Step 4:
Reach out and
grab the word
(to bring all the
sounds back
into the word).

In the Classroom
Multisensory Hand
Spelling

Hand spelling is an activity in which students are taught to raise their thumb as they say the first sound of a word, then extend all four of their fingers out together, like in a handshake, as they say the rest of the word. They can then repeat the whole word, reaching out to grab the sounds while they bring their fingers and thumb back together. This activity highlights onset and rime with the thumb for the sounds that come before the vowel and the stretched-out hand representing the rime chunk. It's great for Phase 1 and 2 spellers and engages all students to listen and say the words. In Phase 4 hand spelling is helpful in helping students focus on phonics chunks when spelling words by analogy such as *-ake*, *-ight*, *-oat*, and the like.

D. The week's words are used in traditional phonological awareness activities, such as picture matching or sorting by initial sound and oral phonemic blending and segmentation tasks such as finger spelling or Elkonin boxes. Finger spelling is a step beyond hand spelling that highlights each sound within a word; here students still hold up a thumb for the initial sound but now extend their pointer finger for the second sound and another individual finger for each subsequent sound as they develop awareness at the level of the phoneme. They reach out and pull all the fingers back in after they stretch through the word, blending the sounds together. Remember this is still all aural.

Day 2 and Day 3

The second and third days of the week share a common lesson plan, but with different words used on each day, pulled from the original weekly word set. The weekly block of words is divided in half: half the words will be used on Day 2, the other half on Day 3. We recommend you use easily decodable words on Day 2 and more complex or less regular words on Day 3 (we provide guidelines for forming blocks of words later in the chapter).

Where Day 1 was devoted solely to Hear-It and Say-It activities, the lessons for Days 2 and 3 target all five steps. The lessons start with a repetition of teacher and student stretching through the sounds of the day's words. Hand spelling and/or finger spelling can be used again to increase student engagement and promote phonological awareness during this Hear-It and Say-It warm-up. In the next step, Write-It, the teacher engages the students in a spelling dictation activity, in which the students are instructed to simply try their best to spell each word as they hear it or see it in their mind. They are repeatedly reminded that this is not a test. When presented in this way, students see this as a fun, engaging activity. There are no wrong responses at this point.

Note right away how this differs from traditional spelling instruction. There is no memorization of an assigned word list. There is no test of recall or formal summative assessment that is scored and graded at this point. Instead, there is a listening-first stimulation, a linking of speech and hearing, and a student-directed process of generating a spelling—from within.

In the Classroom

Elkonin boxes

Elkonin boxes, named after Russian Psychologist D. B. Elkonin, are small boxes placed below a picture that guide a child in sound segmenting. In the original task, students move a token or slide their finger into each box for each sound within a word, as they listen to and say the word.

Recall from the previous chapter how a student's self-generated spelling offers a window into their literacy development. The Phase Theory described in Chapter 5 allows you to now obtain a clear picture of each student's development. The spelling that students produce is very revealing indeed—it will let you estimate their phase of development and give you an idea of their phonological awareness and understanding of the alphabet. But that is not all—a student's spelling provides a developmentally appropriate starting point for explicitly teaching reading. This is done through a teacher-led discussion and structured feedback about the word's spelling.

Essentially, following the student spelling activity the teacher undertakes the process of moving the spelling to a conventionally correct form. There is more than one way to do this depending

In the Classroom
Teacher Talk—
Implementing a Spell-to-Read Approach

"When spelling with my students I always let them know that I am not interested in only correct spellings; I'm interested in knowing what they hear and how they *think* words are spelled. Because if I can see what they are thinking, it's easier for me to move them to the correct spelling of words. I tell them I don't want them to worry about being right or wrong and feeling like they should copy what their friends are writing because if they do that they are only showing me what their friends hear and think. I want to know what they think."

—A grade 1 teacher, on using a spell-to-read approach

on the setting (individual, small group, whole class). For class-level instruction, the teacher can lead a discussion of the specific sounds and spelling of the word as she guides the students to compare their own spelling to the conventionally correct one. In small groups or with individual work, the teacher is able to more directly guide the students' spelling to another level with individualized feedback. In all situations the key is to make the experience a highly metalinguistic one—that is, one where there is an explicit awareness of sound and language. This is done through a discussion of the sound-letter correspondences in the word (and the student's spelling)—a discussion of what patterns match expectations and what parts may come as a surprise for the given word. It is, in essence, a conversation about spelling. The degree of personalized feedback given to each student will depend on the class or group size, but these principles remain the same: it should always be an engaging metalinguistic experience.

The lessons for Days 2 and 3 conclude with other reading and writing activities that incorporate the words students have just heard and spelled. This is the Use-It grand finale of the planned lessons. Words can be used for other isolated word study and practice, read in context through guided and independent reading, or included in writing activities. In this way, the words are incorporated into other ongoing literacy activities already established in your classroom.

Day 4 and Day 5

On the final days of the week, the same general lesson plan is followed (from Days 2 and 3), but now the teacher selects some words from Day 2 and some from Day 3 to work on together. Recall that we recommend using decodable, regular words for Day 2 lessons and high-frequency sight words that may vary in regularity/consistency on Day 3. Days 4 and 5 include an opportunity to mix the words— this highlights to the student that words differ in how easily they can be decoded/encoded, but that a sounding out strategy is still the best starting point regardless. This metalinguistic approach helps student generalize their developing literacy skills across words of all types and is what integrates the routes to reading. Remember, we're working to increase orthographic learning in an effort to establish them as brain words—regardless of regularity/consistency.

Teacher Feedback to Student Spelling

The principles of the listening-first, spell-to-read approach can be applied within any setting, from individual or small groups to the entire class. The feedback provided by the teacher will of course depend upon the group or class size. Guidelines are given next for different applications.

Large Groups/Classroom Instruction

Following the initial auditory bombardment, familiarization, and having students attempt the spelling, the correct spelling can be shown (e.g., on the board or Smart Board). Alternatively, invite willing students to share their spelling or have the class provide the spelling for you to write— letter by letter—by asking what the start of the word is, what comes next, and so on. In all cases, direct the students to compare the correct spelling to their own, sound by sound, letter by letter. Discuss the sounds made by the letters and highlight anything surprising about how the word is spelled. Stretching through the word with moving targets can be especially helpful here. End by having the students copy the correct spelling and then add the next step, Read-It, by having students repeatedly read the word aloud.

TERMINOLOGY TACKLED:

Word Regularity

A word is considered *regular* if it follows expected letter-sound correspondence rules or expectations and *irregular* if it violates these expectations. For example, *cat* is regular because the short vowel is expected in closed syllables (consonant-vowel-consonant as in CVC or CVCC), although *pint* is irregular because it is pronounced with a long vowel where a short vowel would be expected. Consistency refers to variability across words. *Cat* is also consistent because the *at* sequence is pronounced the same way across similar words (e.g., *fat, hat, mat*); *pint* is inconsistent because the same letter sequence is pronounced differently in different words (e.g., *mint*). It has been estimated that about half of all words in English are regular and consistent. And most of the others only have one deviation—meaning that they can be spelled phonetically with only one error. Only about 5 percent of English words are truly irregular (Hanna et al. 1966; Moats 2005/2006). This is why a listening-first, sounding out strategy is the best starting point—for all word types.

Smaller Groups/Individual Instruction

With smaller groups, it is possible to give more personalized feedback to each student. This fits especially well with remedial work and early Response to Intervention tiers already in place within the school. The regular classroom can also be organized to allow for small-group work that can integrate our approach.

With smaller groups, individualized feedback can be given to each student. Here, a five-rung feedback progression can serve as a useful guide.

In the Classroom
Teacher Talk— Implementing a Spell-to-Read Approach

"In my class, students each have a small dry-erase board and marker. After students have created their spelling attempt, I invite someone who wants to share their attempt to do so on the Smart Board or class board, and I go through any corrections that need to be made, sound by sound, letter by letter. Then students share their spellings by holding up their boards. I ask everyone to write the word three times to help store the correct spelling in their brain (regardless if they correctly spelled on first attempt so weaker spellers don't get demoralized). We then all read the word together several times."

> —An elementary school resource teacher on using spell-to-read in the classroom and with larger groups.

1. Verify if the initial sound is represented. If not, stretch through the word, emphasizing the first sound, and ask the student to think of what the first sound is.

2. Verify the final sound is represented. If not, stretch through the word, emphasizing the final sound, and ask the student to think of what the final sound is. If the final sound is a vowel, discuss how the vowel sound is spelled in this case.

3. Verify the medial sounds (if the word has more than two sounds). This may be a good time to discuss how all words need a vowel. Note too that there may be more than one medial sound (e.g., *u* and *m* in *jump*). If a medial sound is missing, stretch through the word, emphasizing the missing sound, and ask the student to think of that sound.

4. Now discuss any spelling patterns specific to the word, to shape the correct brain representation of the word. Discuss the number of sounds and the number of letters in the word (sometimes they will be the same—as in simple CVC words like *cat*; often they do not match due to silent letters, vowel teams, digraphs, etc.—as in words like *screamed*).

5. Have the student copy the correct the spelling and read the word repeatedly.

Note that these feedback guidelines are the most straightforward progression for single-syllable words. As words become more complex, the same principles apply—focus on each part of the word sequentially, beginning with the starting sounds and then focus on the ending sounds, because these are the most easily processed in hearing and memory. Then tackle the interior of the word.

In the Classroom
Elkonin Boxes for Additional Spelling Practice

Elkonin boxes can be used as an additional Use-It spelling activity. Here, instead of marking each box with a token or sliding their fingers, the students spell the word by placing the letters that make each sound into each box. This is also an excellent way for students to further use speech and hearing pathways as they stretch through the words to spell them.

| P | I | G |

| F | I | SH |

As children move through the developmental phases (see Chapter 5) you can focus on more sophisticated word parts such as syllable types. Individualized feedback such as this gives you the opportunity to match your focus to your student's developmental phase; you can nudge him forward in development by focusing on a missing element, sound, or spelling convention in the next phase of the student's journey. This is precisely how the developmental phases described in Chapter 5 can help inform your approach to teaching reading.

A Word About Word Selection

The words used in your structured weekly lessons can be pulled from a variety of sources if done carefully. The key is to remember that we are integrating the decoding and word reading routes: we treat decodable regular words (often associated with phonics programs) and so-called sight words (often associated with whole word approaches) in the same manner. Brain words are created through orthographic learning, which is kick-started by initial decoding regardless of word type. And because the goal is to make all words brain words, each week should include both easily decodable and less regular/consistent words. Consider this—words are not separated by regularity/consistency in texts, so why keep them separated in teaching?

As stated earlier, after auditory bombardment and familiarization on the first day, we recommend regular decodable words be initially explored on Day 2 and high-frequency words of lesser regularity/consistency on Day 3. Then on subsequent days, they are mixed together to integrate the routes to reading and to promote generalization of literacy skills (Days 4 and 5).

You may already have a district- or school-mandated word list for phonics or spelling and another for establishing high-frequency sight words. If so, you are good to go—just select a few words from each list to target each week. Alternatively, you may have a phonics, spelling, or word sort program in the classroom that you can pull words from to compile your weekly word list of regular decodable words. This is especially beneficial if these are words that your students are going to be exposed to in other literacy activities; by using the same words in our spell-to-read lessons, you can help promote a deeper level of processing and knowledge for these words. High-frequency words can also be taken from one of the commonly used lists easily found online (e.g., Dolch, Fry). The total number of words used each week will depend upon your students, but four to six of each (decodable and high-frequency) is typically an adequate starting point for planning.

If you are starting from scratch in devising a list of decodable words, it can be helpful to keep in mind that many words in English are composed of six basic syllable patterns:

- closed syllables, often thought of as short vowels (e.g., *cat, wig, stop*)
- final *e* syllables, often thought of as long vowels (e.g., *cake, bike*)
- vowel-team syllables, also thought of as long vowels (e.g., *brain, team*)
- open syllables, with no final consonant (e.g., *me*, first syllable of *behind*)
- vowel + *r* syllables (e.g., *far, or*)
- consonant + *le* (e.g., *bubble table*)

You'll probably want to stick with one or two syllable patterns per week at first. As more syllable patterns are included over time, you can incorporate word sorts as an additional Use-It activity. But only after the words have been introduced and practiced following the five-step sequence of a listening-first, spell-to-read approach. As we'll discuss in the next chapter, an excellent source for words is a research-based spelling book. This can give you more confidence that syllable types are presented in a developmentally appropriate sequence.

In the Classroom

The Week's Lesson Sequence in Recap

To recap, here is how the listening-first, spell-to-read five-step sequence maps onto a typical week of structured, planned word study:

- **Day 1.** Hear-It, Say-It for all of the week's words.
- **Day 2.** Hear-It, Say-It, Spell-It, Read-It, Use-It for the week's regular decodable words.
- **Day 3.** Hear-It, Say-It, Spell-It, Read-It, Use-It for the week's irregular and other high-frequency words.
- **Days 4 and 5.** Hear-It, Say-It, Spell-It, Read-It, Use-It for a mix of words taken from Days 2 and 3; teacher's choice and optional assessment.

Student Assessment

The analytic process of listening-first, spell-to-read approach integrates speech and hearing, phonological awareness, reading, and spelling. The spelling process itself and subsequent reading further integrate both analytic and synthetic skills as students begin to map words into their internal lexicon—that is, their own personal dictionary of brain words. Note that your student work samples containing their spelling practice become ready-made portfolio assessment material that documents progress in development; more traditional summative assessment can also be incorporated at the end of each week at the teacher's discretion.

If you desire a more formal posttest assessment, keep in mind that it should be done in much the same way as outlined previously, rather than testing your students' abilities to take home and memorize a word list. Again, here is where we connect phase assessment to teaching. A simple "spell what you hear or think" dictation task provides a ready-made summative assessment. The Monster Test can be used, or words from the teaching progression just outlined can be posttested. The important thing to remember is that the spellings need not be scored as correct or incorrect or used for a grade—especially in kindergarten and first grade. Rather, they can be scored developmentally, as outlined in the previous chapter, to reflect the developmental phase of the student. This allows you to monitor progress at a much more fine-tuned level than would be possible with simple dichotomous correct-or-incorrect assessment grading.

Districts and schools may decide how best to approach the question of how to formally grade spelling in the context of spell-to-read methodology. In general, we recommend that no letter grades be given in kindergarten. In kindergarten it is appropriate to report spelling as being "developmentally appropriate," "below expected development," or "above expected development" along with the phase level. The teacher would report Phase 0, 1, 2, 3, or 4 followed by "on grade level," "below grade level," or "above grade level" as best fits each child during a grading period.

In cases where schools or districts use research-based spelling books with weekly summative assessments, it's acceptable to report the results to parents in the form of a numerical or letter grade but always including the child's developmental phase. This provides a more valid account of how the child is truly developing as a speller, reader, and writer rather than simply how well the child retained words for a weekly test.

Spell-to-Read Implemented During a Teachable Moment

The principles of our listening-first, spell-to-read approach to teaching word reading can also be implemented incidentally in everyday classroom activities, regardless of the program or approach being used in the classroom. Words can be taken from ongoing activities and resources from across your learning day and used with the five-step sequence of our spell-to-read method. Activities can be built into the day, added as a reading center, or delivered to the whole class. If a leveled reader series is used, for instance, appropriate words might be pulled from those books. Care should be taken to ensure the word complexity is grade appropriate and not one that may cause confusion in terms of the spelling pattern (see Chapter 4). Engage the class in metalinguistic discussions of a word's spelling. Point out expected and surprising spelling patterns. Engage hearing and speech in getting students to stretch through the words with hand and finger spelling. And use the words in some extra spell-to-read guided work with the students. We always recommend presenting word study in a positive manner, as an engaging hands-on analytic task. Remember, we are teaching spelling and promoting development, not assigning words to be memorized for a spelling grade. Students enjoy taking the lead in analyzing and thinking about words, coming up with the spelling from within. And as described earlier, this gives you a natural, developmentally appropriate starting point in moving students forward and helping them establish brain words.

In the Classroom
A Word About Word Walls

The widespread use of word walls is frequently based on the myth that children can magically learn to read from mere exposure to print. The vast majority of children require explicit teaching—and exposure to words pinned on the wall isn't explicit teaching. In general word walls may be too passive to instantiate meaningful learning, and they can actually confuse students if great care is not taken to ensure word selection follows developmentally appropriate spelling patterns and the right high-frequency words are introduced at the right time. We recommend adding words to word walls only after they have been used with listening-first, spell-to-read instruction.

Words from children's own writing are often an excellent source for finding words to explore in more focused word study using our five-step sequence. Misspelled words in writing often tell you which high-frequency words or spelling patterns the children already know or do not know. When working with individuals, simply choose appropriate words from a child's writing and engage her in a meaningful, metalinguistic discussion of spelling. Recall that a sentence or two generally includes a large enough sample of invented spellings to determine the child's phase; this can serve as a ready-made source of words to explicitly teach by bringing hearing, speech, spelling, and meaning together in highly metalinguistic discussions. And when these domains come together, brain words can be built.

Keep in mind how incorporating the principles of our listening-first, spell-to-read method into daily practice can be as simple as engaging in a discussion of spelling as words are encountered. Any language and literacy activity that involves listening and speaking can be broadened to include increased awareness to spelling. In sum, there are essentially no programs or approaches into which the principles of a spell-to-read method and our five-step sequence cannot be integrated—to the benefit of all students.

In the Classroom

Brain Words Link Sound, Spelling, Meaning

Research supports the importance of linking meaning with sound and spelling in creating brain words. This is evident in everyday classroom practice too. In a humorous real-world example, a classroom teacher we know introduced a new lesson on cursive writing to her class. One of her students asked for clarification. "What are we doing?" he asked. "Cursive writing," replied the teacher. "Please write *Cursive Writing* as the title on the front of your notebook." When the students handed in their notebooks, she laughed out loud when she saw what that student had written: *Curse of Writing!* Then she noticed another student had done the same. *The Curse of Writing!* This humorous story illustrates how in analyzing spoken language, we match the sounds we hear to representations that exist in our memory for words we already know in our spoken language system. These kids knew *curse of* but not *cursive!* The lesson to take away: always make sure students understand the word you are asking them to spell. This way they can anchor the pronunciation and spelling and meaning all together for a high-quality, complete brain word

In the Classroom

Teacher Talk— Implementing Spell-to-Read Principles Daily in Kindergarten

"Before reading a new story, big book, text, or flip chart poem, I tell the students they are going to hear some words today. I may pick only two words, one irregular and one good sound-matching word. We will say the words several times, both slowly, stretching the sounds at a natural rate, and use the words in sentences. I then ask if anyone wants to come up and try to spell that word like a grown-up might. In correcting the spelling, I identify any correct letter and use the phrasing 'just like you I hear the "__" sound'; conversely, if I have to change a letter I say, 'Here the "__" sound is made by the letter(s) __.' We talk about how many sounds and letters are in the word. I invite the kids to spell the correct spelling on their imaginary whiteboards. They do this by printing the word in the air. After we have done both words, I read the story. I encourage anyone who hears or sees the word when I'm reading to flash their fingers like a flashbulb."

—A kindergarten teacher about building principles of spell-to-read into other activities.

CHAPTER 7

Building Brain Words in Second Through Sixth Grade

With the practices we presented in the previous chapter in mind, let's explore how to build brain words beyond first grade: what's the same, what's different, and what adjustments are needed for utilizing a spell-to-read approach to reading instruction in second through sixth grades? Then with a good grounding in spell-to-read methodology, let's see how connecting building brain words to vocabulary, meaning, and oral language continues to support effective comprehension and meaning making with older readers and what the research says about efficient resources and techniques for building brain words. Chapter 7 ends with very specific effective learning techniques from cognitive psychology that apply directly to building brain words in second grade through sixth grade

Remarkably, the process for adding brain words in second grade through sixth grade is the same as discussed in the previous chapters except that, typically, the brain's Word Form Area is already well established and ready to add more word spelling knowledge to the other components of word identity (sound and meaning) represented in the dictionary in the brain. There are no more "developmental stages" that change the brain's architecture, only many more words and concepts to add to the dictionary that already exists. In effect, orthography—that is to say, spelling—activates the child's language system and uses it for reading comprehension and fluent writing.

A Brief Review: All Children Must Go Through the Developmental Phases

We begin with a brief review of what has happened in kindergarten and first grade to get brain words in place and ready for success in second grade and beyond. As shown in Chapter 5, students are expected to progress through five developmental phases of spelling and reading and begin to show evidence of orthographic learning and the storage of brain words before entering or at the beginning of second grade. Ideally, students will arrive in the upper grades having successfully moved through the early developmental phases, but if they haven't, you will need to take a step back and meet them where they are with special intervention. Here's a recap of how second graders should have moved through five research-based developmental phases beginning in preschool.

In preschool, there was no dictionary in the brain for reading and writing (unless the child was a precocious early reader), that is to say, no neuroimaging evidence of an established Word Form Area to support reading (see Chapter 3). But as children move through the kindergarten and first-grade phases, the reading brain begins to develop its circuitry as children engage with reading and writing fostered by good teaching. In Phase 1, kindergarten children begin to visually perceive and process alphabet letters—they learn to write their names, identify some letters, and even recognize a few words based on environmental cues. With appropriate reading and writing instruction the kindergartner's brain begins to change some more.

The move to Phase 2 evokes further brain changes as alphabetic symbols (letters) start to be matched to stored representations for sounds and at the same time speech codes are being connected with pronunciations in the child's spoken language along with higher-order language skills for sentences and comprehension. In Phase 3, often in the first half of first grade, brain changes help children decode words with one-to-one letter-to-sound mapping and encode or spell words with sound-to-letter mapping as the sounding out route to reading develops.

Then the magic happens. In Phase 4 the developing Word Form Area begins to store phonics chunks and words for automatic retrieval. The chunks include high-frequency long and short vowel patterns, some affixes such as –s and –ing, at least five of the basic syllable types, and meaning-based word parts such as the *in* and *to* in *into*, the *can* and *not* in *cannot*. It's in this consolidated/automatic alphabetic Phase 4 that the Word Form Area begins to show up in neuroimaging and at the same time self-teaching kicks in (and that's probably why it seems like "magic"), orthographic learning takes off, and the routes to reading become intertwined. So that by the end of first grade (for some kids early in second grade) the complex reading brain circuitry is basically in place with a dictionary of chunks of phonics patterns and words: for end-of-first graders perhaps three to four hundred brain words are stored in their lexicon—their internal dictionary in the brain—that can be retrieved automatically for reading and writing. Some were placed there in earlier phases as decodable words with frequent use and with self-teaching became automatically recognized brain words. Others were learned in spelling or word study lessons. The neurological reading circuit, which was not present at birth, is in evidence by the start of second grade, and it is connected to higher-order cognitive functioning such as feelings, language, and thought. Once children have passed through the five phases of early development, they are ready for building brain words in second through sixth grade.

Spell-to-Read Methodology in Second Through Sixth Grade

The Hear-It, Say-It, Write-It, Read-It, Use-It elements in the spell-to-read lesson sequence outlined in Chapter 6 are built into the process of specifically building brain words in second through sixth grade with the same systematic spelling method. But now our spell-to-read five-step sequence is compressed, and all steps are encapsulated within a spelling pretest on the first day of a weekly spelling unit.

Step 1   Students initially engage in an auditory or listening *Hear-It* process
as the teacher pronounces each word on a spelling pretest.
Note that students hear the pretest word before seeing it.
This is not a test of memorization.

Step 2   Students *say it*, pronouncing the word out loud based on teacher
modeling. Remember all of this is happening aurally. The students
have not yet seen the pretest words in print. Be sure to give students
an opportunity to connect each word to sound and meaning in their
spoken language system by giving them pretest sentences; these
sentences help students decide how they think the word is spelled
in meaningful context. This enables the students to apply connecting
the word to a word they use in speaking.

In the Classroom

Hear-It, Say-It, Write-It, Read-It, Use-It on the Pretest

Here's an example of a third-grade weekly lesson on single-syllable homophones that highlights our spell-to-read five-step sequence on a pretest: The teacher would first pronounce the pretest word *sell* so the students can *hear it*. Then the children repeat the word out loud, activating phonology as they *say it*. Next the teacher uses the word in a sentence such as "Mrs. Sands wants to *sell* her car." This helps the students connect the spelling pretest word to sound and meaning in their own spoken language system. Now they *write it* as they think the word should be spelled. Finally they self-correct their attempt as they *read it* from a model of the correctly spelled word. Beginning this day and for the remainder of the week students will practice the new word as they *use it* in various activities. This same five-step sequence would be used with the other words in this lesson such as the words *sail* (with a sentence such as "It is fun to *sail* a boat"), and *cell* (with a sentence such as "The robber was put in a prison *cell*"). By self-correcting each word after analyzing their attempted spelling against the correct model, students begin to *learn* the correct spelling and make the spelling-meaning connection within their own spoken language circuitry. (Lesson adapted from Gentry 2012.)

Step 3 The progression continues with a written attempt on the pretest as students try their best to spell each word as they hear it or see it in their mind associating this pretest word with what they already know. This is their initial attempt to *write it*.

Step 4 Word analysis begins with the next step where the children are shown the correct spelling for the first time and read the word from the correct model. This is the *Read-It* component, and as they read the word, they self-correct by comparing their own spelling with the correct model.

Step 5 Now students are ready to use the correct spelling in the *Use-It* component of the five-step sequence. After the pretest students are given strategic opportunities to use the spelling words meaningfully in speech, often working with peers to practice using them in sentences.

It's important to reiterate that the words second through sixth graders are learning to spell should be words in their own spoken language by the end of this first lesson. In other words, you want to make sure that this is a word they know and can use orally before expecting them to spell it correctly on a final test.

As the week continues, give students multiple opportunities to re-present the words in their brains based on the five-step building-a-brain-word sequence introduced in Chapter 6 and utilized on Day 1 during the pretest. Students continue throughout the week with mixed activities incorporating the Hear-It, Say-It, Write-It, Read-It, Use-It progression, though not always going through the full five-step sequence each day. Options for the remainder of the week might include multisensory activities such as a Look-Say-See-Write-Check "flip folder" multisensory word study technique (see the In the Classroom box), digital practice options for in school or home practice, meaningful workbook pages, online spelling games, and word-sorting options.

For the remainder of the week students actively engage with the words and make connections by

In the Classroom

The Flip Folder Multisensory Word Study Technique

The flip folder technique is used to study words *after* the words have been presented aurally on the pretest. This Look-Say-See-Write-Check-

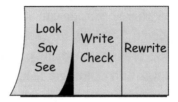

Rewrite multisensory research-based procedure helps students study and learn words that were missed on the pretest.

- Have the student prepare a list of words to be studied by writing them in a column on the left-hand margin of a sheet of paper to be slipped under the flaps. Make sure all the words to be practiced are spelled correctly. The words to be studied will be under the Look—Say—See flap. The sheet under the other two flaps is blank, allowing the students to write their responses by lifting those flaps.

- The student opens the first flap and *looks* and *says* the first word. Then he closes the flap and visualizes the word in his mind's eye, trying to *see* it.

- Now the student lifts the second flap and attempts to *write* the word correctly from memory. The student then lifts the first flap to *check* his spelling.

- Finally, the student closes the first two flaps and lifts the third flap to *rewrite* the word again for additional practice, and then he *checks* it by lifting the first flap.

(Procedure adapted from Gentry 2016e)

using the words being studied in reading and writing. In doing so, students begin to add the spelling for the week's words to their own internal dictionary in the brain permanently. This methodology is very much in contrast to simply assigning a word list on Monday and having students memorize the spelling for the Friday test only to misspell the word later in their independent writing. What's different is that this process builds permanent brain words!

Note that words on the weekly spelling list should be organized by pattern or a spelling principle. The words should also be on the student's instructional spelling level, that is, the level where he or she can already spell about half of the pretest words correctly in a traditional twenty-word weekly list (Morris, Nelson, and Perney 1986). Some research-based programs present pattern- or rule-based lists with on-grade-level, above-grade-level, and below-grade-level designated words to assist teachers in individualization even when working with whole groups. Presenting a pattern list with some words that children can already spell helps them associate their unknown spellings (words misspelled on the pretest) with known words that have the same pattern or spelling principle—words they already know and spell correctly on the pretest. In effect, having some known spellings on the list helps learners build new knowledge onto what they already know. Finally, keep your lists brief. Learning twenty unknown words each week can be too challenging; learning ten or so new brain words each week, along with the principles that allow for transfer to other words that work the same way, is very doable.

After the first day's pretest (self-testing), which is the initial step for engaging the brain, you can spend the rest of the week revisiting the words through the research-based techniques that follow in this chapter. But, before we jump directly into that research, let's take a moment to explore the connection between building brain words and the expanding vocabulary of children in second through sixth grade.

Continue to Connect Building Brain Words to Vocabulary, Meaning, and Oral Language

As we look forward to how research supports building the dictionary in the brain specifically in second through sixth grades, it's important to remember that brain words should be developing in concert with children's spoken vocabulary. Earlier, we discussed how brain words map onto the meaning-based oral language and vocabulary children developed both before entering school and as they move through kindergarten and first grade. By the time they hit second or third grade, children acquire an impressive oral vocabulary estimated to be tens of thousands of words, and this number is expected to continue to grow throughout elementary school. As we turn our focus to second through sixth grades, students fuse the process of developing brain words with their continually evolving oral language and vocabulary. In other words, brain words and vocabulary are interconnected, both working together to help students beyond first grade build on what they've learned to develop more fluent reading and deepen their comprehension. With these integral processes in mind, it's imperative that we give these older students ample opportunities to acquire a strong oral language and deeper vocabulary.

Though children acquire spoken vocabulary in various ways—by viewing and listening to media, by engaging interactively with academic instruction in school, and of course through social interaction—vocabulary growth through these methods is limited. The real secret to building students' vocabularies in second through sixth grades is motivating them to read more. Because children's books have more "rare" words than the conversations of most college graduates (Shaywitz 2003, 106), it turns out that the best way to develop an enormous vocabulary is by reading. In fact, students who read twenty minutes a day process a whopping 1.8 million words a year in the dictionary in their brains (Shaywitz 2003). In essence, every time students read a word, that word is *re-presented* in the dictionary

In the Classroom
Extending the Matthew Effect to All Students

When you consider that vocabulary is built from reading, and those with strong vocabulary tend to be strong readers, and stronger readers read more, then it reasons that a "rich-get-richer" situation is brewing. Children who are reading well have more brain words, they read more, learn more vocabulary and brain words, and hence read even better. The problem is that the opposite may be the case for students who struggle, resulting in a continuously widening gap between strong and struggling readers across the elementary school years. This has been dubbed the "Matthew Effect" (see Stanovich 2009). And this is precisely why intentional, scientifically based teaching is so key: by encouraging reading and delivering systematic spell-to-read instruction to develop brain words, we can help all students "get richer."

In the Classroom

Don't Forget About the Importance of Morphology!

It's important to include heavy doses of morphology (the study of word parts that carry meaning) in spell-to-read word study. Morphological study incudes root words (the primary meaning part of a word such as the Latin root **cycl** in **cycl**e, bi**cycl**e, **cycl**one, and en**cycl**opedia), base words that stand on their own for receiving prefixes and suffixes, compound words, and contractions. Morphological study begins in kindergarten as students learn to make the base word *dog* plural by adding *s* or to add *ed* and *ing* suffixes to verbs. Kindergarten- and first-grade morphology may even include compound words such as *into* and contractions such as *don't*. As students advance through the grades, spell-to-read morphological study intensifies including new opportunities for building new vocabulary that can fascinate students especially with Greek and Latin forms. For example, a whole-class scavenger hunt with the Latin root *jud* can reap new words such as ad**jud**ge, ad**jud**icate, in**jud**icious, **jud**ge, **jud**icial, mis**jud**ge, pre**jud**ice, and many more! Note how morphological spell-to-read study offers many opportunities to connect brain words to phonological awareness and pronunciation as in changing pronunciations of *jud* depending on its position in the word.

in their brains, so the more they read, the more their vocabulary grows, optimizing their comprehension by igniting their connections between oral vocabulary and brain words. Consequently, as children engage in high volumes of reading, they continue to build their vocabulary: they store sound and meaning and have opportunities to store the spelling patterns of read words as well, through self-teaching and orthographic learning as outlined in prior chapters. Time spent reading both in and out of school is important.

Recall that lexical representations— stored word knowledge—consist of sound, meaning, and spelling. As presented throughout this book, systematic spelling practice throughout the elementary grades provides further opportunities to install meaningful word representations to each student's growing internal dictionary or lexicon of sound and meaning. In other words, in the spell-to-read method, you are not only teaching brain words in a way that connects to the spoken language system, you are also completing the learning of new vocabulary by linking sound, meaning, and spelling. For example, students learn *sail*, *cell*, *great*, *grate*, and *sole* and *soul* not only as spelling words but as new vocabulary. Reading success is about activating the reading circuitry and using brain words to connect to a large vocabulary of stored words for comprehension. Systematic spelling practice both activates and completes these stored representations in the brain. The result? Fully specified brain words for subsequent use in reading and writing.

Spelling Instruction: The Missing Piece

Thus far we have outlined how our five-step spell-to-read sequence can be utilized to introduce a weekly spelling unit in second grade and beyond and how important it is to connect spelling to students' oral language systems. The overall message here is clear: intentional and organized spelling instruction can be the missing piece in literacy teaching. Spelling instruction promotes continued growth of reading and writing skills through the elementary school grades, by establishing fully specified lexical representations of sound, meaning, and spelling—the very brain words at the heart of this book. For the remainder of this chapter, we will consider some specifics of spelling instruction.

Utilize a Research-Based Spelling Curriculum

Do you know which students in your classroom are spelling at or above grade level and which ones are below? Do you know what specific word pattern features or spelling principles each student needs to be taught? Systematic stand-alone research-based spelling instruction based on an intentional curriculum ensures that reading circuitry is ignited with phonological knowledge, deep phonics knowledge, morphological knowledge, and vocabulary knowledge necessary for grade-level reading fluency.

In addition to giving you an instructional blueprint so you can begin the year with a plan appropriate for your grade level from Day 1, a grade-by-grade spelling curriculum helps you identify students who haven't learned or aren't learning to spell as expected both within and across grade levels and offers a way for you to monitor each student's spelling progress from one grade to the next.

Weekly spelling pretests based in a specific course of study help you see how each child fares in your grade-level curriculum and can function as an elementary or upper-level spelling inventory, allowing you to identify word pattern features or grade-specific spelling principles that your students know or do not know. The pretest helps you group for teaching spelling and make decisions regarding time spent and focus on particular word or pattern features. Beyond that, a grade-by-grade curriculum brings continuity to the curriculum across grade levels, and in struggling schools where there is often high teacher turnover—as many as three teachers per year in some classrooms—this consistency is imperative.

Unfortunately, as we mentioned in Chapter 4, many schools today lack a research-based spelling curriculum, and teachers are often left their own devices when making one. Because you may not have the expertise (or time!) to create a research-based curriculum on your own and most districts leave spelling instruction so open ended, we highly encourage you to consider research-based spelling books. These books are often the best delivery system for spelling curriculum and instruction, because they're based on developmental theory and research-based principles. You can identify the spelling curriculum of any grade level by just looking at the book's table of contents and save yourself the guesswork around what needs to be taught at a particular grade. Because the word lists are research based, they present the right words at the right time so you can monitor growth and detect difficulties early. These lists often come with options for differentiating the weekly list with on-, above-, or below-grade-level words based on your students' progress. And, because research-based books focus on encoding—which requires deeper learning than phonics or decoding—their curriculum fits well with any reading program.

Failing to provide a grade-by-grade spelling curriculum and explicit spelling instruction with a stand-alone program for upper-grade students—especially those in high-poverty, low-performing schools, or schools with many English language learners—is often a missing piece of literacy instruction and a major reason why so many of our students have difficulty with reading. But remember, this isn't just about spelling. Good spellers tend to be good readers, and many students are poor readers because they can't spell.

 ## Research in Action

A Case for Spelling Books

1. *Spelling books can be used with a spell-to-read methodology as a safety net.* Regardless of which reading or writing curriculum is being used, brain science shows that spelling is foundational for reading (Willingham 2015) and spelling books are research supported above and beyond other delivery systems for teaching spelling (Gentry 2004; Wallace 2006).

2. *A spelling curriculum makes early detection and intervention of reading difficulties more likely.* Noticing an abnormality in a child's spelling development as they move through the curriculum in a spelling book is one of the best indicators for early intervention, which is a key for overcoming dyslexia (Gentry 2006; Texas Education Agency 2014).

3. *Spelling books enable teachers to monitor each student's spelling growth.* Too many schools aren't tracking individual spelling growth because they don't have a grade-by-grade spelling curriculum. Spelling books offer continuity across grade levels for monitoring each student's progress and when needed for providing intervention.

4. *Research-based spelling books go hand in hand with improving reading scores.* Poor reading and poor spelling are directly connected (Adams 1990, 1998; Gentry and Graham 2010; Moats 2005/2006; Reed 2012), and as reported by Wallace (2006) spelling books continue to find support in twenty-first-century research, showing that the skills presented in a research-based spelling book curriculum also promote reading (Graham and Santangelo 2014; Ouellette and Sénéchal 2008; Ouellette, Sénéchal, and Haley 2013; Ouellette, Martin-Chang, and Rossi 2017; Ouellette and Sénéchal 2017).

5. *Spelling books focus on encoding.* Both decoding and orthographic pathways must be engaged for reading, but ultimately words that children learn to decode should become correctly spelled brain words that can be retrieved automatically. Spelling books often help children take words they can read to the deeper level of encoding. Remember, *encoding* (spelling correctly) requires more precision than using phonics alone for decoding and reading (Carreker 2011; Foorman and Francis 1994).

Practice Effective Learning Techniques for Transfer

Effective learning techniques for word permanency in the brain along with transfer into automatic processing for reading and writing is accomplished by following techniques supported by research. Spelling is a highly researched subject area in literacy education, yet practices continue to ignore many

TERMINOLOGY TACKLED:

What Is Word Permanency?

We refer to complete and correct mental representations of words that may be retrieved for both reading and writing as the condition of *word permanency* in the brain. It contrasts with students memorizing a word list for a Friday spelling test but later being unable to retrieve the correctly spelled word when writing. Word permanency combats an age-old problem of a lack of transfer where words were memorized for a spelling test but the same words were later misspelled in writing. Correct mental representations of spelling, or word permanency, help free the brain during the reading process for making connections leading to fluency and comprehension.

effective learning techniques for word permanency and transfer supported by these studies. Next, we explore both traditional practices and newly discovered evidence-based spell-to-read approaches to support second- through sixth-grade learners in building brain words and word permanency.

In a 2006 review of the research titled "Characteristics of Effective Spelling Instruction," Randall Wallace reported the following traditional spelling instructional practices supported by research (Wallace 2006, 276):

- Giving weekly spelling lists and administering weekly tests, as the difficulty of the words is adjusted to the instructional level of the speller.

- Administering words in a pretest-teach-posttest format with students self-correcting the tests as much as possible.

- Including words originating from other subjects and from students' own reading and writing in conjunction with the commercially prepared word lists.

- Keeping records, such as a log, that notes misspelled words offers the student, parent, and teacher a way to isolate and practice words that are personally difficult for a student to spell.

- Teaching strategies and procedures that assist students to learn new words.

To date, there have been no studies refuting the use of these traditional practices for teaching spelling explicitly even though many schools neither have a grade-by-grade spelling curriculum nor follow these traditional practices supported by twenty-first-century research.

Teaching the Six Syllable Types

One of the more recent research-based practices to help students learn new words and transfer those words for automatic reading and writing is focused instruction on six commonly used syllable types in English (Moats 2009; Weakland 2017). Mark Weakland points out that including the typical research-based spelling scope and sequence with focus on the broad six syllable-type categories makes it easier for students to connect what they already know to new learning (Weakland 2017). Including six syllable types in the curriculum makes spelling easier to learn and easier to teach because it challenges the false notion that spelling patterns are always based on overwhelming minute details rather than big picture patterns under broad categories. Recognizing the six syllable types helps children read and spell new words (Moats 2009, Weakland 2017). Here, we specifically name for students and call their attention to the six syllable types—or chunks— that are highly reliable and are used both within and across grade levels: open syllables, closed syllables, vowel-consonant-*e* (CVe), vowel-*r* syllables, vowel team (including diphthongs), and consonant-*le* (C-le) syllables. These easy-to-understand overarching chunking categories appear in students' growing vocabulary of polysyllabic words beginning in first grade and extend into adulthood. The six syllable types were highlighted by Louisa Moats in 2009 but interestingly can also be found in Webster's introduction of spell-to-read methodology in *The American Spelling Book* popularly known as the "Blue-Backed Speller" from 1789!

Five More Teaching Techniques for Word Permanency

Teachers often ask: "What's the best way for my students to learn and retain words from the weekly spelling list? How do I get them beyond simply memorizing words for a Friday spelling test only to forget how to spell the word the next time it pops up in writing?" John Dunlosky and his colleagues (2013) present learning strategies derived from research in cognitive and educational psychology that fit with our spell-to-read approach to teaching. Each of these five strategies (as adapted from Gentry 2016b) helps create brain words.

In the Classroom

The Six Syllable Types Found Within and Across Grade Levels

Open syllables (V, CV, CCV): *me, she, he, no, so, go, to-tal, ri-val, mo-tor*

Closed syllables (VC, CVC, CCV): (about 50 percent in running text) *in, pet, stuff, com-mon, but-ter*

Vowel-consonant-e (VCe): *make, while, poke, puke, ape* (called "*e*-marker" or "silent *e*")

Vowel team syllables (teams may be two, three, or four letters and can represent a long, short, or diphthong vowel sounds): *thief, boil, hay, boat, straw, hey, boy, bough, taught, night*

Vowel-r syllables (numerous, hard to master; they require continuous review): *fir, fur, perform, ardor, mirror, further, wart*

Consonant-le syllables (C-le) (*stable final syllable*, C-le combinations): *puzzle, riddle, quadruple* (Note: there is no doubled consonant as in CC-le. Doubling is caused by combining C-le with a closed syllable.)

1. Take a self-test. Begin study of a weekly unit with a pretest, which is a self-test for spelling. Giving a pretest, followed by a week of various activities for closely examining words that culminate in a posttest, is research-proven best practice (Allal 1997; Wallace 2006). Dunlosky et al. (2013) found self-testing to be one of the most effective learning strategies. It is efficient because it enables the learner to focus on those words that are unknown. And, as discussed earlier, the pretest is also an excellent time to provide a listening-first auditory stimulation and opportunity to link hearing and speech to spelling (our Hear-It, Say-It, Read-It, Write-It, Use-It steps—all in one!).

2. Self-correct the pretest, focusing on each misspelled word, and have the learner ask "how questions." Asking "how questions" such as "*How* does the correct spelling relate to information I already know or what I am learning in this lesson?" is what Dunlosky et al. (2013) call "self-explanation." Often, self-explanation comes into play in lessons that teach spelling rules. In a research-based spelling book, for example, a third grader will learn a few good rules that explain *how* spelling works: "If a word ends in a consonant followed by *y*, the *y* changes to *i* to add any suffix except *–ing* as in *mystery, mysteries*; *carry, carried*; *hurry, hurrying*. If a word ends in a vowel followed by *y*, the base word is unchanged as in *delay, delayed, delays*, and *delaying*" (Gentry 2016e).

3. Have the student question herself and explain "why" she chose a particular spelling. Dunlosky et al. (2013) call asking these kinds of questions "Elaborative Interrogation." After a lesson on homophones, a third grader who learns to spell word pairs such as *great* and *grate, roll* and *role*, or *scent* and *cent* would know them as homophones—two or more words having the same pronunciation but different meanings, origins, and spellings. After the lesson, the student would be able to explain "why" she spelled the homophones to match the meaning. Using terminology such as *homophone*, as in this Elaborative Interrogation example, increases metalinguistic awareness; as established in the previous chapter, metalinguistics play a causal role in literacy learning. Through these first three listed strategies, the students integrate our Hear-It, Say-It, Read-It, Write-It, Use-It steps in a meaningful and engaging manner.

4. Mix up the practice for long-term effects. Dunlosky et al. (2013) call this learning technique "Interleaved Practice." This involves implementing a schedule of practice that mixes different kinds of word study activities within a single study session. In a research-based spelling curriculum, third graders might practice words they missed on the pretest beginning with an auditory analysis and going through our Hear-It, Say-It, Read-It, Write-It, Use-It steps as they compare the word with the correct spelling. On different days of the weekly unit they might do meaningful practice pages, make connections to reading and writing, use online spelling games, or sort words with a buddy as follow-up practices that lead to making the word a brain word. Effective spelling programs incorporate Interleaved Practice by mixing up activities to boost learning.

5. Break up the practice into short sessions throughout the week. This psychologically backed technique is called "Distributed Practice." For spelling, the research recommends breaking up explicit spelling study into short sessions of fifteen minutes per day or sixty minutes spread over the week (Moats 2005/2006). Students leave it and come back to it day after day—but only for a short time.

In the Classroom

The Founding Father of American Education Knew About Brain Words!

Remarkably, the founding father of American education and author of America's first reading program jump-started reading with spelling. More than 200 years before neuroscientists would show that spelling was at the core of the reading brain, Noah Webster's reading program started out with a spelling book (Webster 1789). And most of his syllable patterns are still taught today. It's estimated that 60 million American children learned to read in the 1800s with Webster's blue-backed speller. Yes, Webster's spelling book taught America to read—and his strategy was to begin by teaching brain words and chunks. (See Figure 7.1.)

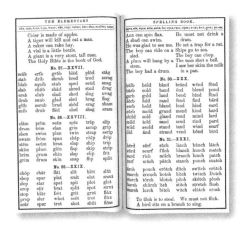

FIGURE 7.1

Webster's Blue-Backed Speller (1789)

Proficient reading—reading with fluency and comprehension—foremost depends upon the ability to read words. And the ability to read words is enhanced through orthographic learning that integrates the routes to reading and completes the reading circuitry in the brain. The result is the activation of the brain's Word Form Area and the establishment of brain words. And spelling instruction is very much the missing link in establishing brain words in the upper elementary grades. If we don't explicitly teach children to spell, their reading brain may not be optimized to its fullest potential. They may suffer in this era of rigorous standards and frequent testing. Dyslexia referrals and the high costs of remediation may increase, and the struggles of English language learners may be further exacerbated. Research-based resources and techniques, used in conjunction with our general spell-to-read principles and five-step sequence, can help students continue to add brain words throughout the elementary school years and beyond.

CHAPTER 8

Understanding and Supporting Children with Dyslexia in Light of Reading Science

Have you ever been told that there is no such thing as dyslexia or that we should call this specific learning disorder by some other name? We have heard imminent reading scholars make such claims, yet dyslexia does exist. True, dyslexia is hard to diagnose, and psychologists, educators, and even scientists in the lab have not developed adequate screening tools or tests for dyslexia. But the fact that dyslexia exists as a biological reality is incontrovertibly demonstrated by cognitive science and neuroimaging as a complicated interruption of the very complex reading circuitry encompassing both pathways to reading. Some scientists report that the decoding-based reading disorder (aka developmental dyslexia) may affect 5 to 10 percent of school-aged children across languages and is actually quite common relative to other neurobiological disorders (Black, Zhichao, and Hoeft 2017). Others report one in five school children may be affected by dyslexia (Shaywitz 2003). Yet schools often fail to diagnose dyslexia correctly (Quinn and Wagner 2013). In this chapter we show you how the science of reading and development of brain words are biologically and innately connected to dyslexia. We will also share some recommendations for your classroom because, without a doubt, dyslexia affects some of the children you teach.

In a nutshell dyslexia is a biologically based condition that makes it difficult for children or even adults to learn to read fluently and spell correctly. In laymen's terms, the typical brain organization for reading and spelling does not function as expected in dyslexia even though the learner may be intelligent and in a stimulating environment. It's important to remember that dyslexia is the most common learning disability and one that has a genetic component. If you have dyslexia, it's likely that others in your family do too. We know boys are more likely than girls to be diagnosed with dyslexia although dyslexia is found in both sexes (Siegel 2006).

Most recent studies associate dyslexia with early difficulties in letter-sound processing when decoding print or sound-to-letter processing when translating what is heard into print by spelling. As such, dyslexia is often described with reference to underlying phonological processing deficits—that is, difficulties with processing the sounds of our language and how they map onto letters, syllables, and word patterns. As you will learn, there can be other underlying deficits as well. We do know that dyslexia is not a lack of visual abilities or dysfunction in visual processing.

If you are a teacher you will probably encounter students with dyslexia. These students are likely to exhibit significant difficulty in your classroom in at least some of the following areas:

- Learning to read
- Learning to spell
- Auditory processing; difficulty processing speech and language in real time to gain understanding
- Learning other languages
- Test-taking skills; difficulty completing tests
- Completing heavy reading assignments
- Remembering people's names and song titles
- Learning math
- Memorizing scripts
- Overall academic success in school

What Students with Dyslexia Can Do and More on What They Have Difficulty With

Students with dyslexia can learn to read and write by reorganizing their reading circuitry in ways that may differ from the typical reading brain. Much scientific literature reports abnormality in dyslexia in areas of the left temporoparietal cortex, or possibly occipitotemporal cortex (Xia, Hancock, and Hoeft 2017), which as we explain in Chapter 3 and in some detail to follow is where the Word Form Area or representations for the dictionary in the brain are situated.

If we look at what is happening with children's spelling development and see abnormal difficulties, it can be a red flag, that is to say, it could be a symptom of dyslexia. Sometimes we can see this as very young children struggle with phonological awareness, have difficulty learning letters, and create unusual spellings during the developmental spelling phases as outlined in Chapters 5 and 6, which might lead to early detection. Often we see signals in older children's abnormal spelling too. And in some cases, individuals with dyslexia may be able to spell but they have difficulty fluently connecting spelling to pronunciation and meaning within their spoken language system. The theoretical and research-based knowledge we share in this book regarding the importance of spelling to read, developing automatic word reading, and memory of spelling representations connected to speech and language are at the very heart of the matter.

There is no question that the dyslexic brain is not fully understood scientifically. There are likely relatively broad language and literacy impairments associated with dyslexia, making for a heterogeneous disorder; in other words, not all cases of dyslexia will look the same. Researchers Lisa and Martin Kronbichler report "there is an ongoing discussion about whether there are qualitative differences in the neuronal mechanisms that underlie dyslexia, meaning that dyslexic symptoms might be based upon slightly diverging 'neuronal subtypes' of dyslexia" (2018, 8). But don't be discouraged; there is a lot that we do know about dyslexia that will help teachers support affected students.

Although no two human brains are exactly alike, there are certain things that individuals with dyslexia often have difficulty with. As a teacher, likely the first thing you'll notice with these students is how severely they struggle learning to read proficiently and spell correctly, with the latter leading to writing difficulties. Beyond that, those with dyslexia may have various degrees of difficulty with articulating words in everyday speech, retrieving words from memory, and remembering facts. All of these can present on a spectrum ranging from mild to moderate to severe. And of course, all of these can be debilitating in school.

KEYPOINT

Watch out for five common indicators of dyslexia:

- Abnormal spelling
- Unusual difficulty with reading
- Trouble articulating certain words
- Difficulty retrieving specific words or expressing what one knows
- Trouble remembering sequences or facts

On the other hand, in some ways dyslexia can be perceived as a gift. It's not unusual to find those with dyslexia to be extraordinary thinkers, readers, writers, and high achievers. Perhaps due to compensating, trying harder, developing resilience, or possible right brain hemisphere advantages—what sometimes is referred to as "thinking out of the box"—some individuals may find advantages within dyslexia. The message to educators and parents is to strive to understand children's strengths and weaknesses and encourage them to be the best learners they can be while building self-efficacy as well as empathy for others.

It is difficult to compile an agreed-upon, complete, science-based list of dyslexia symptoms; with so much confusion surrounding dyslexia, any list you might find could easily be up for debate. It is, however, helpful to consider "classic" symptoms that have been reported (although not necessarily all verified by research). Because every brain affected by dyslexia is different, the generalized list that follows may or may not apply in any given individual. Still, a cluster of these symptoms within or across the age ranges is certainly worth noting (Barton 2015; Shaywitz 2003).

Classic Warning Signs in Early Childhood (Barton 2015; Shaywitz 2003)

- Speech delay (Language doesn't seem to be occurring as it should. Often the child can understand language normally, but expressive language may be delayed.)

- Chronic ear infections

- Delay in establishing a dominant hand

- Confusion with left and right

- Trouble learning to tie shoes

- Odd pronunciations or saying sounds in the wrong sequence (e.g., *pa-sket-ti* (*spaghetti*), *am-i-nal* (*animal*), *em-i-ny* (*enemy*), *a-lu-ni-mum* (*aluminum*)

- Difficulty with word retrieval or trouble finding the word one wants to use (e.g., "that thingy")

- Trouble with rhyming words

- Early difficulty with letter names and sounds

- A history of family members with reading problems

Strengths may include high levels of thinking, imagination, and vocabulary, as well as early artistic, athletic, or manipulative abilities.

Classic Warning Signs in School-Aged Children (Barton 2015; Shaywitz 2003)

- Difficulty memorizing arbitrary sequences such as days of the week and months of the year, or sequences in solving math problems
- Learning multiplication tables
- Misspelling their own name
- Letter and number reversals after first grade
- Learning things such as one's address or phone number
- Continuing difficulties with retrieving the correct word when speaking (e.g., use of "whatchamacallits" and "thingies")
- Issues with directionality (i.e., being left/right confused)
- Issues with dominance (i.e., right-handed or left-handed)
- Poor handwriting skills
- Extremely poor spelling

Classic Warning Signs for Young and Older Adults (Barton 2015; Shaywitz 2003)

- Struggling with academics in school
- Lifelong struggles with spelling
- Fear of reading aloud
- Difficulty with written expression
- Slow reading rate
- Poor test-taking skills
- Difficulty remembering people's names or retrieving known information (e.g., song titles), particularly under duress
- Difficulty learning foreign languages
- Bad sense of direction (e.g., difficulty knowing whether to go left or right when walking out of a hotel elevator at the end of the day; a bad sense of directionality when driving)
- Difficulty reading musical notes from a score

We don't expect that any person with dyslexia experiences all of these symptoms, but a pattern of them should call attention to teachers, parents, and Individualized Educational Plan (IEP) teams.

Bring Your Knowledge of Dyslexia Research Up to Date

To better understand the current research on dyslexia, let's review what we learned in Chapter 2 and recall the two science-based routes to word reading leading to automatic activation of reading circuitry. Words can be read by (1) mapping graphemes (letters) to phonemes (sounds) in the sounding out process of decoding or they can be read by (2) directly accessing the pronunciation (and meaning) of larger letter strings and entire words via the orthographic pathway. Beginning readers start mainly with route 1, the sounding out process. With repeated exposures to the words and instruction, they begin to build a representation of the word spellings in memory as they move through the phases (see Chapter 5) incorporating the words they learn to decode over time into route 2 for automatic recognition. Route 2 emerges from the orthographic learning process, which results in permanent representations of correct spellings or what we call brain words.

As children move through the five developmental phases of reading and spelling, reading circuitry is built and refined. Over time, we see a transition in development to increased reliance on brain words and automatically recognizing correctly spelled words and syllable patterns. This transition is where the routes to reading intersect and they become integrated, which often becomes particularly noticeable for teachers in Gentry's Phase 4 when students begin to read independently easy chapter books such as *Little Bear* at Level H and write with many words spelled correctly as well as unknown spellings invented in logical chunks of phonics patterns.

With dyslexia, early struggles with phonological awareness, decoding, and encoding can directly restrict orthographic learning of brain words and interfere with the expected move through the five phases of development. Children with dyslexia have less successful decoding and encoding, which directly blocks opportunities for orthographic learning and subsequent automatic recognition of brain words. Moreover, brain functioning difficulties with sounding out unfamiliar words or listening to their sounds and inventing a spelling can hinder the establishment of accurate orthographic, that is to say, spelling representations in memory.

The result is an incomplete development of automatically recognized brain words—the much needed detailed orthographic or spelling representations involved in whole word recognition and automatic reading (Share 1995, 1999; Van den Broeck and Geudens 2012).

As if this weren't complex enough, there is more to creating brain words than phonology or speech sounds alone. It is a complex, integrative process where the reading routes must come together to link letter sequences to pronunciation and meaning. But what if the reading routes don't come together? This is what appears to be happening in dyslexia due to a biological dysfunction.

Look again at the model originally presented in Chapter 2, which is represented in Figure 8.1. This shows the expected integration of the two pathways for normal readers.

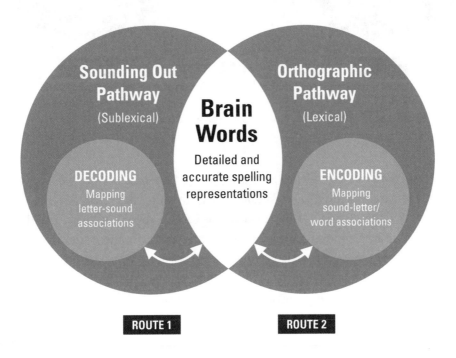

FIGURE 8.1

An Integrated Model for Beginning Reading

Now look at the model again, yet changed to reflect the reality of dyslexia in Figure 8.2. You see the lack of integration and the diminished evidence of brain word development.

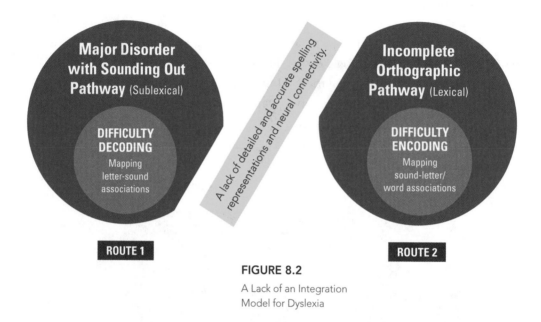

FIGURE 8.2

A Lack of an Integration
Model for Dyslexia

Although phonological processing is a big part of dyslexia, we know from behavioral research, including case studies, that both routes depicted in Figure 8.2 may be associated with dyslexia (Wang, Nickels, and Castles 2015). Children with dyslexia thus may not only have difficulties with phonological awareness and decoding as involved in route 1, they may also struggle with forming detailed orthographic or spelling representations necessary for fluent reading as implicated in route 2 (Share 1995; Ziegler et al. 2003); we propose, as depicted in our revised model in Figure 8.2, that this may often be caused by a lack of integration between the routes to reading in development. This in turn leads to less spelling knowledge and fewer brain words. Essentially, this lack of spelling ability and brain words is the chief reason many with dyslexia have so much difficulty learning to read (Kemp, Parrila, and Kirby 2009; Ziegler and Goswami 2005).

The available literature (e.g., Pugh et al. 2001; Dehaene and Cohen 2011) provides evidence that anomalies in the Word Form Area, where representations for the dictionary in the brain are situated, are closely related to the root of what some refer to simply as reading disorder. We think a better descriptor might be "decoding- and/or encoding-based reading disorder." As science helps us improve the understanding of the cause of dyslexia, perhaps it will lead to more accurate and earlier early detection, enable targeted intervention, and lead to improved outcomes for children at risk (Xia, Hancock, and Hoeft 2017). We think the future looks promising. Importantly, we believe understandings gleaned from this book will help you with early detection, targeted instruction, and more support for the students you teach.

As we think back to Chapters 2 and 3 in the context of dyslexia, imagine what it would be like for a child if the two reading routes could not be integrated due to a neonatal "glitch" in brain development (Shaywitz 2003). That seems to be what happens. Neuroimaging has confirmed that individuals with dyslexia show reduced activation in key brain areas identified in the reading circuit, but even more so, they differ in how well these regions work together (Cao, Bitan, and Booth 2008; Finn et al. 2014). As stated in recent neurological research, "Together, research suggests dyslexia involves more than an underactivation of key brain regions in typical left hemisphere reading networks, but also reduced functional *connectivity* between them" [emphasis added]. (Wise-Younger, Tucker-Drobb, and Booth 2017, 90). This is in essence the neurological reflection of the two routes failing to integrate!

Spell-to-Read and Dyslexia

As just reviewed, dyslexia makes it very difficult to build and retain brain words. People who struggle with dyslexia almost always tend to struggle their whole lives with spelling. And although many people with dyslexia learn to read and can even be superior at comprehension or thinking outside of the box, they do often have reading anomalies such as a slower reading rate and difficulties expressing what they have read and understood verbally.

Difficulties with spelling, gleaned through phase observation (as described in Chapter 5), may be among the first best warning signs of possible dyslexia and can lead to early intervention. In older children and adults knowing the symptoms and recognizing that one may have dyslexia can sometimes even be liberating. In our professional careers we have encountered hundreds of individuals who breathed a sigh of relief when they discover that their learning problems or certain everyday misfires in thinking were nothing more than dyslexia playing tricks on their otherwise perfectly functional brain. Some had pondered for years without knowing that some of the symptoms described in this chapter were byproducts of dyslexia:"Why am I all of a sudden so inarticulate and I can't explain what I'm trying to explain?";"Should I hide the fact that I am a horrible speller?"; "Why can't I think of a longtime acquaintance's name when I run into her in the grocery store?";"Why am I so awful with driving directions?" All of these have been reported as annoyances possibly associated with dyslexia. It's sometimes a relief for students suffering from dyslexia to have a teacher who realizes they aren't stupid or lazy. It's just dyslexia!

Dyslexia cannot be diagnosed by looking at spelling alone. But difficulties with spelling and brain words actually seem to be one of the most overarching symptoms at any age from kindergarten and first grade through elementary school and even into adulthood. And given our spell-to-read focus as the missing link to reading proficiency, we want to take a close look at spelling as a symptom of dyslexia.

It's helpful for all teachers to know the symptoms of dyslexia along with spell-to-read methodology. Symptoms generally fall into two categories: (1) early symptoms in kindergarten and first grade as children are beginning to learn to spell and move through the Gentry developmental phases and (2) symptoms in second grade and above. Interestingly, both categories are very similar and often not difficult to spot: you will be looking for abnormalities in typical development.

Early Symptoms of Dyslexia Observed in Spell-to-Read Methodology

Chapter 5 presents a clear picture of how children go through five developmental phases of spelling in early spelling-to-read development of brain words. Look for children who are *not* following the predicted path. For example, the following samples are from first-grade twins in a family where an older brother experienced difficulties due to dyslexia from first through fifth grade. It should be noted that this family had the advantage of highly educated, extraordinarily positive and involved parents who took charge of their children's education. Having worked collaboratively with Richard for two years, the parents and Richard first saw spelling-to-read differences in the twins in first grade as early as November even though the family was providing much literacy support at home.

The parents and Richard started with a grade-level placement test in November. Largely due to advantages at home, Kaia was already functioning at end-of-first-grade to second-grade level as a speller. Anderson, who had the same advantages at home and the same teachers in school, placed at beginning-first-grade level. But from a spelling-to-read phase observation, the differences were even more revealing than the differences in grade levels. Look at the examples of their November Monster Test scores in Table 8.1 collected by their father. In each column you see the child's spelling followed by a phase level ranking from Phase 2 to Phase 4. It's always typical for there to be one or two outliers, but what's striking here are the overall patterns that help reveal how these children are thinking about how spelling works.

TABLE 8.1

Monster Test scores for Kaia and Anderson

	Word	Kaia—No Symptoms Her Spelling (Phase Score)	Anderson—Symptoms of Dyslexia His Spelling (Phase Score)
1	monster	*monst* (2); *left out /r/*	*moostootr* (3)
2	united	*ynitid* (4)	*unidid* (4)
3	dress	*jres* (4)	*jest* (2); left out /r/
4	bottom	*botum* (4)	*bootum* (4)
5	hiked	*hicked* (4)	*hicht* (3)
6	human	*Hyomin* (4)	*pwmim* (2); left out /h/
7	eagle	*egol* (4)	*igl* (3)
8	closed	*closed* ✓	*codst* (2); left out /l/
9	bumped	*buned* (2); left out /p/	*but* (2); left out /p/
10	type	*tipe* (4)	*tell* (2); left out /ī/ and /p/

Kaia's Monster Test reveals a clear pattern. Seven of her spellings are in Phase 4 plus one word is spelled correctly. This is consistent with her end-of-first-grade to beginning-second-grade spelling instructional level on the placement test. By comparison, Anderson did not seem to be progressing as expected through the developmental spelling phases. His spellings are a conglomeration of Phases 2, 3, and 4 with no discernible cluster of spellings revealing what phase he is in. Rather, his responses were scattered, indicating confusion regarding how he thought the English spelling system works. He made unusual rather than predictable choices such as *pw* for the /h/ sound in *human* and other unexpected choices such as *moostootr* for *monster*, which doesn't seem logical. His spelling of *t-e-l-l* for *type* seems way off base. On the grade-level spelling test administered the same week Anderson demonstrated additional dyslexia symptomatic spellings on the first-grade list: *ool* for *all*, *bo* for *do*, *be* for *he*, and *tew* for *ten*. His parents had previously worked on teaching him some of these higher-frequency words at home, but they had not stuck as brain words. Anderson's atypical spelling patterns and inability to store and retain brain words were all indicators that dyslexia may be a factor.

Fifth Grader Kaden's Symptoms of Dyslexia Observed in Spelling

After years of frustration in school and some successes, Kaden, through the remarkable work and intervention both at school and at home by his parents, and due to his own resilience and hard work, was highly successful in fifth grade—that is to say, with most everything except spelling. He wrote a remarkable piece, which, with teacher-assisted publication, demonstrates his accomplishment as a thinker and writer (see Figure 8.3).

Text of Kaden's Letter

I don't know what I want to be when I grow up. I like to mountain bike, skiing, sailing, and playing soccer. I like sailing the best. I want to be on Team Oracle in America's cup. If I want to do that I think I need to be an engineer.

Some classes I need to take are science (Hydrodynamics, Aerodynamics, and Physics), Math (Measurements of speed, and studying the wind), and Programming. I need to be physically fit. Finally, I need to know my sailing knots and just sail to feel good under pressure. I have been doing that since I was six.

Sincerely, Kaden

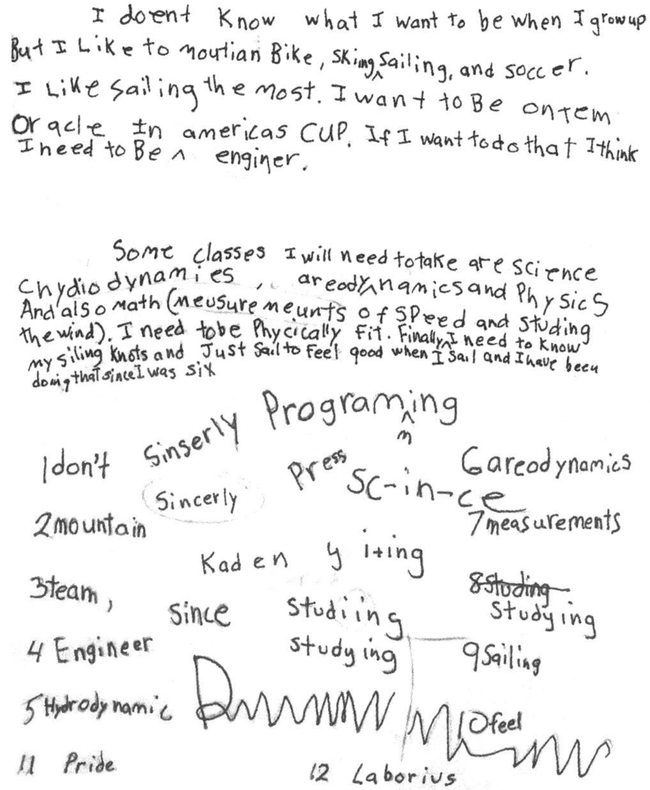

I doen't Know what I want to be when I grow up
But I Like to moutian Bike, SKiing Sailing, and soccer.
I Like Sailing the most. I want to Be on Tem
Oracle in americas CUP. If I want to do that I think
I need to Be ∧ enginer.

Some classes I will need to take are science
(hydio dynamies, areodynamics and Physics
And also math (meusuremeunts of Speed and Studing
the wind). I need to be Phyically Fit. Finally I need to know
my siling Knots and Just Sail to feel good when I Sail and I have been
doing that since I was six

Programing
I don't Sinserly Programing
         (Sincerly)   Press   Sc-in-ce   6 areodynamics
2 mountain   7 measurements

                    Kaden y iting
3 team,   Since   Studiing   8 Studing Studying
4 Engineer   Studying
            study ing   9 Sailing
5 Hydrody namic   10 feel

11 Pride   12 Laborius

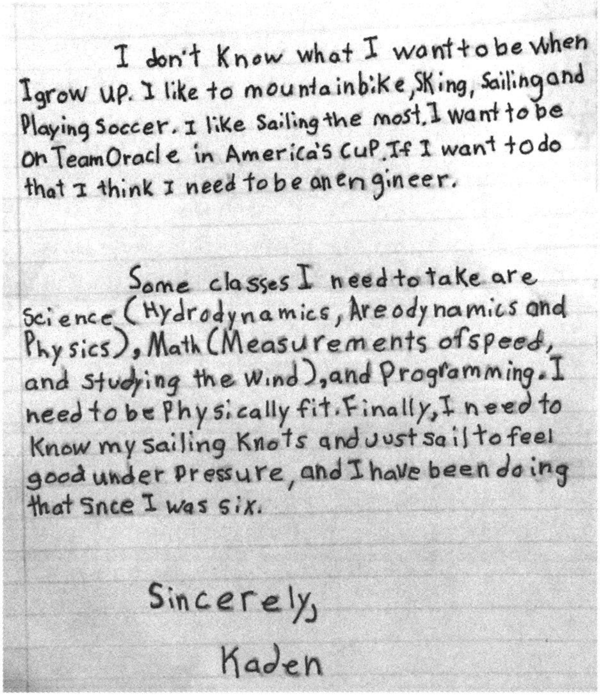

I don't Know what I want to be when
I grow UP. I like to mountain bike, SKiing, Sailing and
Playing Soccer. I like Sailing the most. I want to be
On Team Oracle in America's CuP. If I want to do
that I think I need to be an engineer.

Some classes I need to take are
Science (Hydrodynamics, Areodynamics and
Physics), Math (Measurements of speed,
and Studying the wind), and Programming. I
need to be Physically fit. Finally, I need to
Know my sailing Knots and Just sail to feel
good under Pressure, and I have been doing
that Snce I was six.

Sincerely,

Kaden

FIGURE 8.3

Kaden's Fifth-Grade
Writing and Spelling

We think the letter is extraordinary. Yet Kaden's first-draft spelling was symptomatic of dyslexia: *doent* for *don't*; *moutain* for *mountain*; *tean* for *team*; *Americas* for *America's*; *a* for *an*; *enginer* for *engineer*; *chydiodynamies* for *hydrodynamics*; *areo dynamics* for *aerodynamics*; *meusuremenunts* for *measurements*, *programing* for *programming*, *siling* for *sailing*; *studiing* for *studying*; *feels* for *feel*; *ben* for *been*; and *sinserly* for *sincerely*. As demonstrated here, an accomplished fifth grader who has grappled with dyslexia will often struggle with brain words, syllable patterns, and spelling rules that he or she has been taught. What we admire most about this sample is that, despite dyslexia, we predict Kaden will achieve great things in life thanks in a large part to remarkable parenting, his own positive outlook, and his obvious intelligence.

What Science Says About Interventions

To help children with dyslexia improve their reading skills, phonics-based interventions are usually the first choice; such approaches have been found to be effective for improving accuracy of reading—to some extent (Galuschka et al. 2014). Yet there are still a substantial number of children who show poor response to these types of intervention (Torgesen 2000). Furthermore, the longer-term impact of such teaching interventions is largely unknown (Suggate 2016). Depending on the definition of *effective* and the severity of the initial difficulties, it has been estimated that somewhere between 20 and 40 percent of children with dyslexia may actually fail to improve from intervention (Al Otaiba and Fuchs 2002; Torgesen 2000). This may well be because, as described in this chapter, dyslexia involves more than phonology and phonics; it involves integration of reading routes, orthographic learning, and the establishment of high-quality brain words. Regardless of the previous statistics, we feel that all children who suffer from dyslexia can make progress in overcoming this debilitating learning disability. As we always say to teachers and to parents and even to the children themselves, "Never give up!" In our careers we have even encountered people who overcame dyslexia in adulthood.

That being said, it would seem that focusing solely on phonology and decoding can offer some improvement for reading but not for all and not always completely. Furthermore, we know that spelling problems can persist throughout life (Farmer, Riddick, and Sterling 2002; Maughan et al. 2009). Individuals with dyslexia have particular difficulties with orthographic spellings, and as is the case with Kaden, the fifth grader we discussed previously, they tend to use simple phonological strategies and struggle with more complex words (Kemp et al. 2009). Taken together, these observations all point to the importance of integrating the routes to reading in instruction, allowing the best opportunity for orthographic learning to occur so that brain words can be established. As we have presented in this book, a spell-to-read approach does just that. Interventions for dyslexia would be well served to integrate the practices and procedures we have outlined in Chapters 5 through 7.

Reflecting on these practices, it seems fitting to end our exploration of dyslexia with how parents and schools can help, along with specific recommendations for the classroom. It doesn't have to be daunting or overwhelming. In fact as you read through the following lists, you'll find that supporting those with dyslexia can be fairly easy.

How Parents Can Help

- Understand what dyslexia is.
- See what help is available in school.
- If possible, get a tutor who understands dyslexia.
- Find a school that understands your child's strengths.
- Recognize that dyslexia is not a reflection of intelligence or effort.

How Schools Can Help

- Intervene early.
- Teach phonics, linked to phonological awareness.
- Teach spelling explicitly following the spell-to-read recommendations in this book. Spelling ability and the development of brain words is the locomotive that powers the reading brain.
- Teach writing. Begin teaching writing in preschool and kindergarten.
- Avoid having children at risk of dyslexia copy from the board.
- Teach handwriting including manuscript for beginners and cursive beginning in second grade.
- Embrace repetition because the brain "loves" repetition for developing automaticity in almost every skill.
- Don't ever give up with children who are at risk for dyslexia.

Seven Ways to Accommodate Children with Dyslexia in Regular Classrooms

If you or your IEP team suspects that a child may be dyslexic, consider each of these classroom accommodations (adapted from Gentry 2016d):

1. Allow children who may have dyslexia to demonstrate their competence. All children have strengths, and we should look for them. Children who have dyslexia are known to have difficulty with expressive language, that is to say, trouble retrieving the right words, problems with the "it's on the tip of my tongue" phenomenon, or difficulty organizing their thoughts in conversation. A teacher who understands the child's situation will be patient and understanding and perhaps *look for other ways of expression or alternatives* for demonstrating competence.

2. Change your seating arrangement. Individuals with dyslexia can have difficulty organizing, managing their time, following a teacher's directions, and filtering out background noise. Seating a student with dyslexia closer to the teacher can help them focus on instruction by cutting back on classroom noise and reducing distractions.

3. Use a research-based spelling curriculum and spell-to-read guidelines as a dyslexia-specific intervention. Follow the spell-to-read recommendations that are the core of this book for both beginners and children in elementary school. Because poor spelling is often a telltale sign of dyslexia, monitoring each student's spelling development is often the first strong indicator for early intervention or referral to a specialist for diagnosis. And a spell-to-read approach to teaching reading helps integrate the routes to word reading and promotes orthographic learning and brain words.

4. Teach handwriting. Having difficulty with handwriting is a major symptom of dyslexia, but because teaching handwriting offers benefits for *all* children, it is important to be an advocate for this in schools. Those with dyslexia tend to spell better in cursive because the letters are connected. We agree with handwriting researcher Dr. Virginia Berninger who summarizes her research as follows: "What we're advocating is teaching children to be hybrid writers. Teach manuscript first for reading—it transfers to better word recognition—then cursive for spelling and for composing. Then, starting in late elementary school, touch-typing" (Klass 2016).

5. Expect to give those with dyslexia more help with proofreading for spelling when writing. Avoid criticizing or counting off for spelling errors. What good does it do to tell a fifth grader that he or she could be a better speller? The student likely already knows this! Instead, offer extra support and teach spelling consciousness—the habit of getting help to make sure that spelling is corrected in important pieces of writing that will be shared with other readers.

6. Be sensitive during foreign language study. English spelling with its very difficult system of drawing spelling patterns from many different languages is always a challenge for students who have dyslexia, but foreign languages are often a challenge, too. Some children are studying foreign languages in elementary school. Be sensitive to foreign language study for children with symptoms of dyslexia. Some high schools and many colleges waive some of the foreign language requirements for students with dyslexia.

7. Make appropriate accommodations. Dyslexia results in a slower reading rate. Teachers should be cognizant of slow reading rates when making in-class or heavy homework reading assignments. Enable students with slow reading rates to use books on tape or recordings. Those with dyslexia should get test-taking accommodations for reading rate fluency tests, which are often used in the early school years, and additional time to take other tests including state or district reading assessments.

Be an advocate for children who may be subject to the constraints of dyslexia. Treat any student who may be struggling to acquire literacy skills with compassion rather than mistaking dyslexia as a sign of inferior intelligence or laziness. Be cooperative with parents who suspect their child may be dyslexic.

The classroom accommodations described here should take into account that students with dyslexia also have many strengths. Remember, some experts even suggest those with dyslexia may be gifted and have special talents such as thinking outside of the box and being creative, artistic, and athletic. They may have special difficulties with brain words, but we should strive to help them achieve their goals and be outstanding citizens. People who are or were suspected to suffer from dyslexia have proven to be some of the world's greatest contributors to humanity today and throughout history—Albert Einstein, Steve Jobs, Benjamin Franklin, Cher, Walt Disney, Steven Spielberg, Leonardo da Vinci, Whoopi Goldberg, Thomas Edison, F. Scott Fitzgerald, Agatha Christie, Pablo Picasso, and more sports and media stars than we can count. Many more became outstanding family members, citizens, and members of our communities. If you have a child who is dealing with dyslexia in your classroom, be the special teacher who that child will be grateful to for the rest of his or her life. Use the information in this book to help you get started.

References

Adams, Marilyn, J. 1990. *Beginning to Read: Thinking and Learning About Print.* Cambridge, MA: MIT Press.

———. 1998. "The Three-Cueing System." In *Literacy for All: Issues in Teaching and Learning*, ed. Fran Lehr and Jean Osborn, 73–99. New York: Guilford.

Al Otaiba, Stephanie, and Douglas Fuchs. 2002. "Characteristics of Children Who Are Unresponsive to Early Literacy Intervention: A Review of the Literature." *Remedial and Special Education* 23 (5): 300–316.

Allal, Linda. 1997. "Learning to Spell in the Classroom." In *Learning to Spell*, ed. Charles A. Perfetti, Laurence Rieben, and Michel Fayol. London: Lawrence Erlbaum Associates.

Association for Childhood Education International. 2007. Elementary Education Standards and Supporting Explanation. http://fedora.lib.umd.edu:9641/1903.1/1693, 2018.

Barton, Susan. 2015. Workshop, University of South Alabama, Mobile, AL. November 18, 2015. See also www.BrightSolutions.US.

Baumann, James, David L. Chard, Jamal Cooks, J. David Cooper, Russell Gersten, Marjorie Lipson, Leslie Mandel Morrow, John L. Pikulski, Shane Templeton, Shelia W. Valencia, Catherine Valentino, and MaryEllen Vogt. 2014. *Journeys Common Core.* Boston: Houghton Mifflin Harcourt.

Bear, Donald R., Marcia Invernizzi, Shane Templeton, and Francine Johnston. 1996. *Words Their Way: Word Study for Phonics, Vocabulary, and Spelling Instruction.* Upper Saddle River, NJ: Merrill.

Bhattacharya, Alpana, and Linnea C. Ehri. 2004. "Graphosyllabic Analysis Helps Adolescent Struggling Readers Read and Spell Words." *Journal of Learning Disabilities* 37: 331–348.

Biemiller, Andrew. 2009. *Word Worth Teaching: Closing the Vocabulary Gap.* New York: SRA.

Black, Jessica M., Zhichao Xia, and Fumiko Hoeft. 2017. "Neurobiological Bases of Reading Disorder Part II: The Importance of Developmental Considerations in Typical and Atypical Reading." *Language and Linguistics Compass* 11 (10).

Breen, Mara, Evelina Fedorenko, Michael Wagner, and Edward Gibson. 2010. "Acoustic Correlates of Information Structure." *Language and Cognitive Processes* 25 (7/8/9): 1044–1098.

Brem, Silvia, Silvia Bach, Karin Kucian, Janne V. Kujala, Tomi K. Guttorm, Ernst Martin, Heikki Lyytinen, Daniel Brandeis, and Ulla Richardson. 2010. "Brain Sensitivity to Print Emerges When Children Learn Letter–Speech Sound Correspondences." Proceedings of the National Academy of Sciences Apr 2010, 107 (17): 7939–7944.

Bus, Adriana, and Marinus van IJzendoorn. 1999. "Phonological Awareness and Early Reading: A Meta-Analysis of Experimental Training Studies." *Journal of Educational Psychology* 91: 403–414.

Callens, Maaike, Wim Tops, and Marc Brysbaert. 2012. "Cognitive Profile of Students Who Enter Higher Education with an Indication of Dyslexia." *PLoS ONE* 7: e38081.

Cao, Fan, Tali Bitan, and James R. Booth. 2008. "Effective Brain Connectivity in Children with Reading Difficulties During Phonological Processing." *Brain and Language* 107 (2): 91–101.

Caravolas Marketa, Jan Volín, and Charles Hulme. 2005. "Phoneme Awareness Is a Key Component of Alphabetic Literacy Skills in Consistent and Inconsistent Orthographies: Evidence from Czech and English Children." *Journal of Experimental Child Psychology* 92, 107–139.

Carreker, Susan. 2011. "Teaching Spelling." In *Multisensory Teaching of Basic Language Skills*, ed. Judith R. Birsh, 251–291. Baltimore, MD: Paul Brookes.

Chyl, Katarzyna, Bartosz Kossowski, Agnieszka Debska, Magdalena Łuniewska, Anna Banaszkiewicz, Agata Zelechowska, Stephen J. Frost, W. Einar Mencl, Marek Wypych, Artur Marchewka, Kenneth R. Pugh, and Katarzyna Jednoróg. 2018. "Prereader to Beginning Reader: Changes Induced by Reading Acquisition in Print and Speech Brain Networks." *Journal of Child Psychology and Psychiatry* 59: 76–87.

Clay, Marie M. 1979. *Reading: The Patterning of Complex Behavior.* 2nd ed. Auckland, New Zealand: Heinemann.

———. 1991. *Becoming Literate: The Construction of Inner Control.* Portsmouth, NH: Heinemann.

Cohen, Laurent, and Stanislas Dehaene. 2004. "Specialization Within the Ventral Stream: The Case for the Visual Word Form Area." *NeuroImage* 22: 466–476.

Coltheart, Max. 2005. "Analyzing Developmental Disorders of Reading." *Advances in Speech-Language Pathology* 7: 49–57.

Coltheart, Max, Kathy Rastle, Conrad Perry, Robyn Langdon, and Johannes Ziegler. 2001. DRC: "A Dual Route Cascaded Model of Visual Word Recognition and Reading Aloud." *Psychological Review* 108: 204–256.

Cunningham, Anne E. 2006. "Accounting for Children's Orthographic Learning While Reading Text: Do Children Self-Teach?" *Journal of Experimental Child Psychology* 95: 56–77.

Cunningham, Anne E., Kathryn E. Perry, Keith E. Stanovich, and Paula J. Stanovich. 2004. "Disciplinary Knowledge of K–3 Teachers and Their Knowledge Calibration in the Domain of Early Literacy." *Annals of Dyslexia*, 54: 139–167.

Cunningham, Anne E., Katherine E. Perry, Keith E. Stanovich, and David L. Share. 2002. "Orthographic Learning During Reading: Examining the Role of Self-Teaching." *Journal of Experimental Child Psychology* 82: 185–199.

Dehaene, Stanislas. 2009. *Reading in the Brain.* New York: Viking.

Dehaene, Stanislas, and Laurent Cohen. 2011. "The Unique Role of the Visual Word Form Area in Reading." *Trends in the Cognitive Sciences* 15 (6): 254–262.

Dehaene-Lambertz, Ghislaine, Karla Monzalvo, and Stanislas Dehaene. 2018. "The Emergence of the Visual Word Form: Longitudinal Evolution of Category-Specific Ventral Visual Areas During Reading Acquisition." *PLOS Biology* 16(3): e2004103.

DeWitt, Iain, and Josef P. Rauschecker. 2013. "Wernicke's Area Revisited: Parallel Streams and Word Processing." *Brain and Language* 127 (2):181–191.

Dunlosky, John, Katherine A. Rawson, Elizabeth Marsh, Mitchell J. Nathan, and Daniel T. Willingham. 2013. "Improving Students' Learning with Effective Learning Techniques: Promising Directions from Cognitive and Educational Psychology." *Psychological Science in the Public Interest* 14: 4–58.

Ehri, Linnea C. 1987. "Learning to Read and Spell Words." *Journal of Literacy Research* 19 (1): 5–31.

———. 1991. "Development of the Ability to Read Words." In *Handbook of Reading Research*, ed. Rebecca Barr, Michael L. Kamil, Peter Mosenthal, and P. David Pearson, 2: 383–417. White Plains, NY: Longman.

———. 1997. "Learning to Read and Learning to Spell Are One and the Same, Almost." In *Learning to Spell: Research, Theory and Practice Across Languages*, ed. C. Perfetti, L. Rieben, and M. Fayol, 237–269. Mahwah, NJ: Erlbaum.

———. 2000. "Learning to Read and Learning to Spell: Two Sides of a Coin." *Topics in Language Disorder* 20: 19–36.

———. 2004. "Teaching Phonemic Awareness and Phonics." In *The Voice of Evidence in Reading Research*, ed. P. McCardle and V. Chhabra. Baltimore, MD: Paul Brookes.

———. 2015. "How Children Learn to Read Words." Oxford Library of Psychology. *The Oxford Handbook of Reading*, ed. A. Pollatsek and R. Treiman, 293–310. New York: Oxford University Press.

Ehri, Linnea C., and Sandra McCormick. 2006. "Phases of Word Learning: Implications for Instruction with Delayed and Disabled Readers." *Reading & Writing Quarterly* 14 (2): 135–163. DOI: 10.1080/1057356980140202.

Ehri, Linnea C., Simone R. Nunes, Steven A. Stahl, and Dale M. Willows. 2001a. "Systematic Phonics Instruction Helps Students Learn to Read: Evidence from the National Reading Panel's Meta-Analysis." *Review of Educational Research* 71: 393–447.

Ehri, Linnea C., Simone R. Nunes, Dale M. Willows, Barbara Valeska Schuster, Zohren Yaghoub-Zadeh, and Timothy Shanahan. 2001b. "Phonemic Awareness Instruction Helps Children Learn to Read: Evidence from the National Reading Panel's Meta-Analysis." *Reading Research Quarterly* 36: 250–287. DOI: 10.1598/RRQ.36.3.2.

Ehri, Linnea, and Lee S. Wilce. 1987. "Does Learning to Spell Help Beginners Learn to Read Words?" *Reading Research Quarterly* 22 (1): 47–65.

Farmer, Marion, Barbara Riddick, and Christopher M. Sterling. 2002. *Dyslexia and Inclusion, Assessment and Support in Higher Education.* Dyslexia series. London, UK: Whurr.

Feldgus, Eileen, and Isabell Cardonick. 1999. *Kid Writing: A Systematic Approach to Phonics, Journals, and Writing Workshop.* Chicago: The Wright Group of McGraw–Hill Education.

Feldgus, Eileen, Isabell Cardonick, and J. Richard Gentry. 2017. *Kid Writing in the 21st Century.* Los Angeles: Hameray Publishing Group.

Finn, Amy S., Matthew A. Kraft, Martin R. West, Julia A. Leonard, Crystal E. Bish, Rebecca E. Martin, Margaret A. Sheridan, Christopher F. O. Gabrieli, and John D. E. Gabrieli. 2014. "Cognitive Skills, Student Achievement Tests, and Schools." *Psychological Science* 25 (3): 736–744. DOI: 10.1177/0956797613516008.

Foorman, Barbara R., and David J. Francis. 1994. "Exploring Connections Among Reading, Spelling, and Phonemic Segmentation During First Grade." *Reading and Writing* 6: 65–91.

Friederici, Angela D. 2012. "The Cortical Language Circuit: From Auditory Perception to Sentence Comprehension." *Trends in Cognitive Science* 6 (5): 262–268. DOI: 10.1016/j.tics.2012.04.001. Epub April 18, 2012.

Frith, Uta. 1985. "The Usefulness of the Concept of Unexpected Reading Failure. Comments on Reading Retardation Revisited." *British Journal of Developmental Psychology* 3: 15–17.

Galuschka, Katharina, Elena Ise, Kathrin Krick, and Gerd Schulte-Körne. 2014. "Effectiveness of Treatment Approaches for Children and Adolescents with Reading Disabilities: A Meta-Analysis of Randomized Controlled Trials." *PloS One* 9 (2): e89900.

Gentry, J. Richard. 1977. *A Study of the Orthographic Strategies of Beginning Readers.* Doctoral dissertation. Charlottesville, VA: University of Virginia.

———. 1978. "Early Spelling Strategies." *The Elementary School Journal* 79 (2): 88–92.

———. 1982. "An Analysis of Developmental Spelling in GNYS at Work." *The Reading Teacher* 36: 192–200.

———. 1985. "You Can Analyze Developmental Spelling. *Teaching K–8* 15: 44–45.

———.1987. *Spel . . . Is a Four-Letter Word.* Portsmouth, NH: Heinemann.

———. 2000. "A Retrospective on Invented Spelling and a Look Forward." *The Reading Teacher* 54 (3): 318–332.

———. 2004. *The Science of Spelling: The Explicit Specifics That Make Great Readers, and Writers (and Spellers!),* Portsmouth, NH: Heinemann.

———. 2005. "Instructional Techniques for Emerging Writers and Special Needs Students in Kindergarten and Grade 1 Levels." *Reading & Writing Quarterly* 21: 113–134.

———. 2006. *Breaking the Code: The New Science of Beginning Reading and Writing*. Portsmouth, NH: Heinemann.

———. 2008. *Step-by-Step Assessment Guide to Code Breaking*. New York: Scholastic.

———. 2010. *Raising Confident Readers: How to Teach Your Child to Read and Write—From Baby to Age 7*. New York: Da Capo/Long Life.

———. 2012. *Spelling Connections: Grade 3*. Columbus, Ohio: Zaner-Bloser, Inc.

———. 2015. "Why America Can't Read." *Psychology Today* blog. August 25, 2015.a https://www.psychologytoday.com/us/blog/raising-readers-writers-and-spellers/201707/lousy-spelling-why-americans-can-t-read-or-think.

———. 2016a. "Connecting Spelling Books to Reading Scores: New Research Explains How Spelling Books Increase Reading Scores." *Psychology Today* blog. July 28, 2016. https://www.psychologytoday.com/us/blog/raising-readers-writers-and-spellers/201607/connecting-spelling-books-reading-scores.

———. 2016b. "5 Brain-Based Reasons to Teach Handwriting in School." *Psychology Today* blog

September 15, 2016. https://www.psychologytoday.com/blog/raising-readers-writers-and-spellers/201609/5-brain-based-reasons-teach-handwriting-in-school.

———. 2016c. "5 Reasons Your Child's School Needs Spelling Books." *Psychology Today* blog. April 23, 2016. https://www.psychologytoday.com/us/blog/raising-readers-writers-and-spellers/201604/5-reasons-your-child-s-school-needs-spelling-books.

———. 2016d. "7 Ways to Accommodate Dyslexics in Regular Classrooms." *Psychology Today* blogs. Posted November 15, 2016. https://www.psychologytoday.com/us/blog/raising-readers-writers-and-spellers/201611/7-ways-accommodate-dyslexics-in-regular-classrooms.

———. 2016e. *Spelling Connections*. Columbus, Ohio: Zaner-Bloser, Inc.

———. 2017a. "Landmark Study Finds Better Path to Reading Success." *Psychology Today* blog. March 30, 2017. https://www.psychologytoday.com/us/blog/raising-readers-writers-and-spellers/201703/landmark-study-finds-better-path-reading-success.

———. 2017b. "Lousy Spelling—Why Americans Can't Read or Think Well." *Psychology Today* blog. July 13, 2017. https://www.psychologytoday.com/blog/raising-readers-writers-and-spellers/201707/lousy-spelling-why-americans-can-t-read-or-think.

———. 2018. "Bridging the Gap Between Science and Poor Reading in America." *Psychology Today* blog. May 16, 2018. https://www.psychologytoday.com/us/blog/raising-readers-writers-and-spellers/201805/bridging-the-gap-between-science-and-poor-reading-0.

Gentry, J. Richard, and Steve Graham. 2010. *Creating Better Readers and Writers: The Importance of Direct, Systematic Spelling and Handwriting Instruction in Improving Academic Performance*. Columbus, OH: Saperstein.

Gentry, J. Richard, and Edmund H. Henderson. 1978. "Three Steps to Teach Beginning Readers to Spell." *The Reading Teacher* 31(3): 632–637.

Gentry, J. Richard, and Jean Wallace Gillet. 1993. *Teaching Kids to Spell.* Portsmouth, NH: Heinemann.

Gimenez, Paul, Nicolle Bugescu, Jessica M. Black, Roeland Hancock, Kenneth Pugh, Masanori Nagamine, Emily Kutner, Paul Mazaika, Robert Hendren, Bruce D. McCandliss, and Fumiko Hoeft. 2014. "Neuroimaging Correlates of Handwriting Quality as Children Learn to Read and Write." *Frontiers in Human Neuroscience* 8 (155). DOI: 10.3389/fnhum.2014.00155.

Goodman, Kenneth S. 1986. *What's Whole in Whole Language?* Portsmouth, NH: Heinemann Educational Books.

———. 1967. "Reading: A Psycholinguistic Guessing Game." *Journal of the Reading Specialist* 6 (4): 126–135.

Goodman, Kenneth, E. Brooks Smith, Robert Meredith, and Yetta Goodman. 1987. *Language and Thinking in School: A Whole-Language Curriculum.* Katonah, NY: Richard C. Owen.

Goodman, Yetta M., Dorothy J. Watson, and Carolyn L. Burke. 1987. *Reading Miscue Inventory: Alternative Procedures.* New York: Richard C. Owen.

Gough, Phillip B., and William E. Tunmer. 1986. "Decoding, Reading, and Reading Disability." *RASE: Remedial & Special Education* 7: 6–10.

Gough, Phillip B., and Connie Juel. 1991. "The First Stages of Word Recognition." In *Learning to Read—Basic Research and its Implications*, ed. Laurence Rieben, Charles A. Perfetti, 47–56. Hillsdale, NJ: Erlbaum.

Graham, Steve, and Michael Hebert. 2011. "Writing to Read: A Meta-Analysis of the Impact of Writing and Writing Instruction on Reading." *Harvard Educational Review* 81 (4): 710–744.

Graham, Steve, and Tanya Santangelo. 2014. "Does Spelling Instruction Make Students Better Spellers, Readers, and Writers? A Meta-Analytic Review." *Reading and Writing* 27 (9): 1703–1743.

Hanford, Emily. 2018. "Rethinking How Students with Dyslexia Are Taught to Read." National Public Radio Education. March 11, 20186:00 AM ET. https://www.npr.org/sections/ed/2018/03/11/591504959/rethinking-how-students-with-dyslexia-are-taught-to-read.

Hanna, Paul R., Jean S. Hanna, Richard Hodges, and Edwin Rudorf. 1966. *Phoneme-Grapheme Correspondences as Cues to Spelling Improvement.* Washington, DC: U.S. Department of Health, Education, and Welfare.

Harm, Michael W., and Mark S. Seidenberg. 2004. "Computing the Meanings of Words in Reading: Cooperative Division of Labor Between Visual and Phonological Processes." *Psychological Review* 111 (3): 662–720.

Henderson, Edmund H. 1981. *"Learning to Read and Spell: The Child's Knowledge of Words."* DeKalb, IL: Northern Illinois University Press.

———. 1990. *Teaching Spelling.* 2nd ed. Boston: Houghton Mifflin.

Henry, Marcia K. 1989. "Children's Word Structure Knowledge: Implications for Decoding and Spelling Instruction." *Reading and Writing: An Interdisciplinary Journal* 2: 135–152.

James, Karen H., and Laura Englehardt. 2012. "The Effects of Handwriting on Functional Brain Development in Pre-Literate Children." *Trends in Neuroscience and Education* 1 (1): 32–42.

Jones, Cindy D., and D. Ray Reutzel. 2015. "Write to Read: Investigating the Reading-Writing Relationship of Code-Level Early Literacy Skills." *Reading & Writing Quarterly* 31: 279–315. DOI: 10.1080/10753569.2013.850461.

Joshi, R. Malatesha, Emily Binks, Lori Graham, Emily Dean, Dennie Smith, and Regina Boulware Gooden. 2009. "Do Textbooks Used in University Reading Education Courses Conform to the Instructional Recommendations of the National Reading Panel?" *Journal of Learning Disabilities* 42: 458–463.

Juel, Connie. 1988. "Learning to Read and Write: A Longitudinal Study of 54 Children from First Through Fourth Grades." *Journal of Educational Psychology* 80: 437–447.

Kemp, Nenagh, Rauno K. Parrila, and John R. Kirby. 2009. "Phonological and Orthographic Spelling in High-Functioning Adult Dyslexics." *Dyslexia* 15: 105–128. DOI: 10.1002/dys.364.

Kilpatrick, David A. 2015. Essentials of Assessing, Preventing, and Overcoming Reading Difficulties. Hoboken, New Jersey: John Wiley & Sons.

Klass, Perri. 2016. "Writing to Learn." *New York Times*, June 21, D6.

Kronbichler, Lisa, and Martin Kronbichler. 2018. "The Importance of the Left Occipitotemporal Cortex in Developmental Dyslexia." *Current Developmental Disorders Reports* 5 (1): 1–8. DOI: 10.1007/s40474-018-0135-4. Epub January 19, 2018.

Kuhl, Patricia K., Barbara T. Conboy, Sharon Coffey-Corina, Denise Padden, Maritza Rivera-Gaxiola, and Tobey Nelson. 2008. "Phonetic Learning as a Pathway to Language: New Data and Native Language Magnet Theory Expanded (NLM-e)." *Philosophical Transactions of the Royal Society B: Biological Sciences* 363 (1493): 979–1000.

Kuhn, Melanie, and Steven A. Stahl. 2003. "Fluency: A Review of Developmental and Remedial Practices." *Journal of Educational Psychology* 95: 3–22.

Landi, Nicole, Charles Perfetti, Donald Bolger, Susan Dunlap, and Batrbara Foorman. 2006. "The Role of Discourse Context in Developing Word Form Representations: A Paradoxical Relation Between Reading and Learning." *Journal of Experimental Child Psychology* 94: 114-33.

Lilienfeld, Scott, Steven J. Lynn, and Laura L. Namy. 2018. *Psychology: From Inquiry to Understanding.* New York: Pearson.

Lonigan, Chistopher, Stephen Burgess, and Jason Anthony. 2000. "Development of Emergent Literacy and Early Reading Skills in Preschool Children: Evidence from a Latent-Variable Longitudinal Study." *Developmental Psychology* 36: 596–613.

Martin-Chang, Sandra, Gene Ouellette, and Linda Bond. 2017. "Differential Effects of Context and Feedback on Orthographic Learning: How Good Is Good Enough?" *Scientific Studies of Reading* 21: 17–30.

Maughan, Barbara, Julie Messer, Stephen Collishaw, Andrew Pickles, Margaret J. Snowling, William Yule, and Michael Rutter. 2009. "Persistence of Literacy Problems: Spelling in Adolescence and at Mid-life." *Journal of Child Psychology and Psychiatry* 50 (8): 893–901.

Maurer, Silvia Brem, Felicitas Kranz, Kerstin Bucher, Rosmarie Benz, Pascal Halder, Hans-Christoph Steinhausen, and Daniel Brandeis. 2006. "Coarse Neural Tuning for Print Peaks When Children Learn to Read." *NeuroImage* 33 (2): 749–758.

Moats, Louisa. 2005/2006. "How Spelling Supports Reading and Why It Is More Regular and Predictable Than You May Think." *American Educator* 29: 12–22.

———. 2009. *Spellography for Teachers: How English Spelling Works (LETRS Module 3)*. Boston: Sopris West.

———. 2018. "How Children Learn to Spell." https://www.scholastic.com/teachers/articles/teaching-content/how-children-learn-spell/.

Monzalvo, Karla, and Ghislaine Dehaene-Lambertz. 2013. "How Reading Acquisition Changes Children's Spoken Language Network." *Brain and Language* 127 (3): 356–365.

Morris, Darrell, Laurie Nelson, and Jan Perney. 1986. "Exploring the Concept of 'Spelling Instructional Level' Through the Analysis of Error-Types." *The Elementary School Journal* 87 (2): 180–200. http://www.jstor.org/stable/1001358.

National Assessment of Educational Progress. 2017. Report on 2017 Reading Results from NAEP website. https://www.nationsreportcard.gov/reading_math_2017_highlights/.

National Institute of Child Health and Human Development, NIH, DHHS. 2000. "Report of the National Reading Panel: Teaching Children to Read: Reports of the Subgroups (00-4754)." Washington, DC: U.S. Government Printing Office.

New York City Department of Education. 2018. *Pre-K–2 Framework for Early Literacy*. New York: NYCDOE Publication.

Ouellette, Gene. 2010. "Orthographic Learning in Learning to Spell: The Roles of Semantics and Type of Practice." *Journal of Experimental Child Psychology* 107: 50–58.

Ouellette, Gene, and Jill Fraser. 2009. "What Exactly Is a Yait Anyway: The Role of Semantics in Orthographic Learning." *Journal of Experimental Child Psychology* 104: 239– 251.

Ouellette, Gene, Sandra Martin-Chang, and Maya Rossi. 2017. "Learning from Our Mistakes: Improvements in Spelling Lead to Gains in Reading Speed." *Scientific Studies of Reading* 21: 350–357.

Ouellette, Gene, and Monique Sénéchal. 2008. "Pathways to Literacy: A Study of Invented Spelling and Its Role in Learning to Read." *Child Development* 79: 799–813.

———. 2017. "Invented Spelling in Kindergarten as a Predictor of Reading and Spelling in Grade 1: A New Pathway to Literacy, or Just the Same Road, Less Known?" *Developmental Psychology* 53: 77–88.

Ouellette, Gene, Monique Sénéchal, and Allyson Haley. 2013. "Guiding Children's Invented Spellings: A Gateway into Literacy Learning." *Journal of Experimental Education* 81: 261–279.

Ouellette, Gene, and Talisa Tims. 2014. "The Write Way to Orthographic Learning: Printing Versus Typing in Spelling Acquisition." *Frontiers in Psychology* 5. DOI: 10.3389/fpsyg.2014.00117.

Peha, Steve, and J. Richard Gentry. 2013. "5 Learning Techniques Psychologists Say Kids Aren't Getting." *Psychology Today* blog. https://www.psychologytoday.com/us/blog/raising-readers-writers-and-spellers/201307/5-learning-techniques-psychologists-say-kids-aren-t

Perfetti, Charles A. 2001. "Reading Skill." In *International Encyclopedia of the Social and Behavioral Sciences*. Walter Kintsch, Cognitive Science Editor. The Netherlands: Kluwer.

———. 2007. "Reading Ability: Lexical Quality to Comprehension." *Scientific Studies of Reading* 11 (4): 357–383.

———. 2011. "Phonology Is Critical in Reading: But a Phonological Deficit Is Not the Only Source of Low Reading Skill." In *Explaining Individual Differences in Reading: Theory and Evidence*, ed. Susan A. Brady, David Braze, and Carol A. Fowler, 153–171. New York: Psychology Press.

Pinel, John P.J. 2018. *Biopsychology.* 10th ed. New York: Pearson.

Plaut, David C., James McClelland, Mark S. Seidenberg, and Karalyn Patterson. 1996. "Understanding Normal and Impaired Word Reading: Computational Principles in Quasi-Regular Domains." *Psychological Review* 103: 56–115.

Primary National Reading Strategy. 2006. *Phonics and Early Reading: An Overview for Head Teachers, Literacy Leaders and Teachers in Schools, and Managers and Practitioners in Early Years Settings.* UK, London: Department of Education and Skills. http://studylib.net/doc/8836766/phonics-and-early-reading--an-overview.

Pugh, Ken R. 2006. "A Neurocognitive Overview of Reading Acquisition and Dyslexia Across Languages." *Developmental Science* 9(5), 448–450.

Pugh, Ken R., W. Einar Mencl, Annette R. Jenner, Jun Ren Lee, Leonard Katz, Stephen Frost, Sally Shaywitz, and Bennett Shaywitz. 2001. "Neuroimaging Studies of Reading Development and Reading Disability." *Learning Disabilities Research & Practice* 16: 240–249. DOI:10.1111/0938-8982.00024.

Purcell, Jeremy J., Xiong Jiang, and Guinevere F. Eden. 2017. "Shared Orthographic Neuronal Representations for Spelling and Reading." *NeuroImage* 147: 554–567.

Quinn, Jamie M., and Richard K. Wagner. 2013. "Gender Differences in Reading Impairment and in the Identification of Impaired Readers: Results from a Large-Scale Study of At-Risk Readers." *Journal of Learning Disabilities* 20 (10): 1–13.

Read, Charles. 1970. "Pre-School Children's Knowledge of English Phonology." *Harvard Educational Review* 41: 1–34.

———. 1975. *Children's Categorization of Speech Sounds in English.* National Council of Teachers of English Research Reading No. 17. Urbana, IL: National Council of Teachers of English.

———. 1986. *Children's Creative Spelling.* London: Routledge & Kegan Paul.

Reed, Deborah K. 2012. *Why Teach Spelling?* Portsmouth, NH: RMC Research Corporation, Center on Instruction.

Reutzel, D. Ray. 2015. "Early Literacy Research: Findings Primary-Grade Teachers Will Want to Know." *The Reading Teacher* 69 (1): 14–24.

Routman, Regie. 1991, 1994. *Invitations: Changing as Teachers and Learners K–12.* Portsmouth, NH: Heinemann.

———. 2000. *Conversations: Strategies for Teaching, Learning, and Evaluating.* Portsmouth, NH: Heinemann.

Sanchez, Cladio. 2018. "The Gap Between the Science on Kids and Reading, and How It Is Taught." *National Public Radio Education.* February 12, 2018, 6:01 AM ET. https://www.npr.org/sections/ed/2018/02/12/582465905/the-gap-between-the-science-on-kids-and-reading-and-how-it-is-taught.

Seidenberg, Mark. 2017. *Language at the Speed of Sight: How We Read, Why So Many Can't, and What Can Be Done About It.* New York: Hatchette Book Group.

Shahar-Yames, Daphna, and David Share. 2008. "Spelling as a Self-Teaching Mechanism in Orthographic Learning." *Journal of Research in Reading* 31: 22–39.

Share, David. 1995. "Phonological Recoding and Self-Teaching: Sine Qua Non of Reading Acquisition." *Cognition* 55 (2): 151–218. DOI: 10.1016/0010-0277(94)00645-2.

———. 1999. "Phonological Recoding and Orthographic Learning: A Direct Test of the Self-Teaching Hypothesis." *Journal of Experimental Child Psychology* 72 (2): 95–129.

———. 2004. "Orthographic Learning at a Glance: On the Time Course and Developmental Onset of Self-Teaching." *Journal of Experimental Child Psychology* 87: 267–298.

Sharp, Anne C., Gale Sinatra, and Ralph Reynolds. 2008. "The Development of Children's Orthographic Knowledge: A Microgenetic Perspective." *Reading Research Quarterly* 43 (3): 206–226.

Shaywitz, Sally. 2003. *Overcoming Dyslexia: A New and Complete Science-Based Program for Reading Problems at Any Level.* New York: Alfred A. Knopf.

Siegel, Linda S. 2006. "Perspectives on Dyslexia." *Paediatrics & Child Health* 11 (9): 581–587.

Stanovich, Keith E. 2009. "Matthew Effects in Reading: Some Consequences of Individual Differences in the Acquisition of Literacy." *Journal of Education* 189 (1–2): 23–55.

Suggate, Sebastian P. 2016. "A Meta-Analysis of the Long-Term Effects of Phonemic Awareness, Phonics, Fluency, and Reading Comprehension Interventions." *Journal of Learning Disabilities* 49 (1): 77–96.

Texas Education Agency. 2014. *Dyslexia Handbook.* Austin, TX: Texas Education Agency. http://www.region10.org/r10website/assets/File/DHBwithtabs10214.pdf.

Torgesen, Joseph K. 2000. "Individual Differences in Response to Early Interventions in Reading: The Lingering Problem of Treatment Resisters." *Learning Disabilities Research & Practice* 15 (1) 55–64.

Tunmer, William, Michael Herriman, and Andrew Nesdale. 1988. "Metalinguistic Abilities and Beginning Reading." *Reading Research Quarterly* 23 (2): 134–158. DOI: 10.2307/747799.

Van den Broeck, Wim and Astrid Geudens. 2012. "Old and New Ways to Study Characteristics of Reading Disability: The Case of the Nonword-Reading Deficit." *Cognitive Psychology* 65 (3): 414–456.

Vellutino, Frank R., Donna Scanlon, Edward R. Sipay, Sheila Small, Rusen Chen, Alice Chen, and Martha B. Denkla. 1996. "Cognitive Profiles of Difficult-to-Remediate and Readily Remediated Poor Readers: Early Intervention as a Vehicle for Distinguishing Between Cognitive and Experiential Deficits as Basic Causes of Specific Reading Disability." *Journal of Educational Psychology* 88: 601–638.

Waldie, Karen, Ann Wilson, Reece Roberts, and David Moreau. 2017. "Reading Network in Dyslexia: Similar, Yet Different." *Brain and Language* 174: 29–41.

Wallace, Randall R. 2006. "Characteristics of Effective Spelling Instruction." *Reading Horizons* 46 (4): 267–278.

Wang, Hua-Chen, Anne Castles, Lindsey Nickels, and Kate Nation. 2011. "Context Effects on Orthographic Learning of Regular and Irregular Words." *Journal of Experimental Child Psychology* 109: 39–57.

Wang Hua-Chen, Lindsey Nickels, and Anne Castles. 2015. "Orthographic Learning in Developmental Surface and Phonological Dyslexia." *Cognitive Neuropsychology* 32 (2): 58–79.

Weakland, Mark. 2017. *Super Spellers.* Portland, ME: Stenhouse.

Webster, Noah. 1789. *The American Spelling Book.* Boston: Isaiah Thomas and Ebenezer Andrews.

Werker, Janet, and Richard C. Tees. 2002. "Cross-Language Speech Perception: Evidence for Perceptual Reorganization During the First Year of Life." *Infant Behavior and Development* 25 (1): 121–133.

Willingham, Dan. 2015. *Raising Kids Who Read: What Parents and Teachers Can Do.* San Francisco: Jossey-Bass.

Wise-Younger, Jessica, Elliott Tucker-Drobb, and James R. Booth J. 2017. "Longitudinal Changes in Reading Network Connectivity Related to Skill Improvement." *NeuroImage* 158: 90–98.

Woo, Elaine. 1997. "How Our Kids Spel: What the Big Deel?" *Los Angeles Times*, May 29, A1.

Xia, Zhichao, Roeland Hancock, and Fumika Hoeft. 2017. "Neurobiological Bases of Reading Disorder Part I: Etiological Investigations." *Language and Linguist Compass* 11 (4): e12239.

Ziegler, Johannes C., and Usha Goswami. 2005. "Reading Acquisition, Developmental Dyslexia, and Skilled Reading Across Languages: A Psycholinguistic Grain Size Theory." *Psychological Bulletin* 131 (1): 3–29.

Ziegler, Johannes C., C. Perry, A. Ma-Wyatt, D. Ladner, and G. Schulte-Körne. (2003). "Developmental Dyslexia in Different Languages: Language-Specific or Universal?" *Journal of Experimental Child Psychology* 86 (3): 169–193.

Index

brain words *(continued)*
    quality, 14
    as reading instruction goal, 48
    science and research on, 3–4
    sound, spelling, and meaning in, 104
    spell-to-read approach and, 5, 30–32
Brem, Silvia, 41
Broca's area, 38
Broeck,Geudens, 129
Burgess, Stephen, 14
Burke, Carolyn L., 54
Bus, Adriana, 21

C

Cao, Fan, 131
Caravolas, Marketa, 52
Cardonick, Isabell, 24, 51, 82–84
Castles, Anne, 130
cerebral cortex, 34–35
"Characteristics of Effective Spelling Instruction"
    (Wallace), 118
child spelling. *See* invented spelling
Chyl, Katarzyna, 39
Clay, Marie, 53–54
closed syllables, 119
close look writing assessment, 82–84
Cohen, Laurent, 24
Coltheart, Max, 16
Common Core State Standards, 48, 50, 57
compound words, 114
comprehension
    in early literacy, 20
    as reading instruction goal, 47–48
consistency, word, 96, 97, 100–101
consolidated/automatic alphabetic phase, 64, 73,
    108–109
    Monster Test analysis and, 79
consonant-le syllables, 119
constructivist language practices, 49
context, three cueing system on, 54
contractions, 114
conventional spelling, 79
correct spelling. *See* conventional spelling

creative spelling. *See* invented spelling
cueing system, 53–56
Cunningham, Anne E., 25, 46, 54
curriculum selection, 115–117
cursive writing, 138

D

decodable words, 96
decoding, 8, 43
    deeper phonics knowledge and, 68
    developmental phases and, 68–69
    developmental theory and, 21–22
    dual-route model and, 18–19
    dyslexia and, 124, 136–137
    self-teaching hypothesis, 25–26, 41, 55
    serial *vs.* sight word reading, 15–20
    sight word instruction and, 26–27
    sight word reading *vs.*, 20
    whole language instruction and, 49
    word walls and, 24
Dehaene, Stanislas, 24, 36, 39, 40, 41, 48, 49, 50, 51, 131
Dehaene-Lambertz, Ghislaine, 36, 41
developmental reading theory, 4, 8, 15, 20–25
    dual-route model and, 18
    language development and, 37–38
    literacy development and, 13
    phase observation and, 10
    phase observation and early spelling to read, 63–85
    phonological awareness and, 52
    on second through sixth grade, 107–109
    on transition from sounding out, 24–25
DeWitt, Iain, 37
dictionary building in the brain, 1–12.
    See also brain words
    definition of, 2
    effective, 3–4
    science and research on, 3–4
dual-route model, 16–17
    definition of, 16
    developmental theory and, 20–25
    dyslexia and, 128–131, 137
Dunlosky, John, 119, 120, 121
dyslexia, 11, 123–140

Monzalvo, Karla, 36, 41

morphology, 114

Morris, Darrell, 112

multisensory approaches, 52–53
  flip folder technique, 111
  hand spelling, 93, 94

Murray, Donald, 50

N

Namy, Laura L., 33, 36

National Assessment of Educational Progress
  (NAEP), 1, 13

National Institute of Child Health and Human
  Development, 20, 47–48, 52

National Reading Panel, 20, 47–48, 50, 52

Nelson, Laurie, 112

neurological reading circuit, 5, 15, 33–43, 88
  defining, 39–41
  development of, 109
  invented spelling and, 65
  Word Form Area in, 39–41

New York City Department of Education, 64, 70

Nickels, Lindsey, 130

non-alphabetic phase, 64, 70, 108

nonwords, 28

O

occipital lobe, 35–36, 38, 124

one-letter-for-a-sound strategy, 72–73, 108

open syllables, 119

oral language. *See* language; speech

orthographic learning, 121
  brain words and, 43
  definition of, 3
  dyslexia and, 128–131, 136–137
  increased reliance on, 41–42
  phonological awareness and, 52
  as reading instruction goal, 48
  self-teaching hypothesis, 25–26, 41, 55
  sight word reading and, 19
  spell-to-read and, 29–32
  whole language instruction on, 50
  word regularity/consistency and, 96

orthography, 28
  definition of, 16

Ouellette, Gene, 25, 28, 54, 55, 57, 64, 117

output buffer, 17–18

P

parietal lobe, 35–36, 38, 124

Parrila, Rauno K., 130, 137

partial alphabetic phase, 64, 71, 78, 108

Perfetti, Charles, 14, 27, 54

Perney, Jan, 112

phase observation, 10, 63–85
  analysis of spellings and, 76–79
  consolidated alphabetic phase, 22–23
  definition of, 64
  dyslexia and, 128–136
  early assessment of, 74–81
  in everyday writing, 82–84
  full-alphabetic phase, 22
  identifying interventions needed through, 64
  literacy development and, 65–69
  monitoring brain changes through, 42
  power of, 66–67
  research supporting, 64
  in spell-to-read, 102
  spell-to-read approach and, 84, 95
  text levels and, 85

phonetic spelling. *See* full alphabetic phase

phonics. *See also* decoding
  analytic *vs.* synthetic, 53
  balanced literacy and, 59
  brain words and, 52–53
  consolidation of knowledge in, 68
  in current teaching practices, 51–53
  current teaching practices on, 9
  definition of, 7, 52
  in early literacy, 20
  pathway to reading, 15
  phonological awareness *vs.*, 7
  as reading instruction goal, 47–48
  self-teaching hypothesis, 25–26, 41, 55
  sight word reading *vs.*, 15–20
  whole language instruction on, 50

root words, 114
Rossi, Maya, 29, 117
rote memorization, 88
running records, 53–56

S

Sanchez, Cladio, 46
Santangelo, Tanya, 29, 117
scaffolding, 6, 89
Schulte-Körne, Gerd, 136
seating arrangements, 138
Seidenberg, Mark S., 18, 46
self-teaching hypothesis, 25–26, 41, 55
    literacy phases and, 68, 108–109
self-testing, 120
semantic cues, 53–54
semiphonetic spelling. *See* partial alphabetic phase
Sénéchal, Monique, 28, 57, 64, 117
Shahar-Yames, Daphna, 28
Share, David, 15, 25, 28, 41, 55, 129, 130
Sharp, Anne C., 59
Shaywitz, Sally, 48, 113, 123, 126–127, 131
Siegel, Linda S., 124
sight word instruction, 8, 25–26
    decoding and, 26–27
    spell-to-read and, 88–91
sight word reading, 15–20
    development of, 23
    dual-route model and, 18–19
    word walls and, 24
sight words, definition of, 26
Sinatra, Gale, 59
Smith, Brooks, 56
Snow, Catherine, 46
sounding out, 24–25
sound spelling. *See* invented spelling
speech
    brain regions involved in, 37
    connecting brain words and, 112–115
    whole language instruction and, 49–50
spell-checkers, 60
spelling, 8. *See also* brain words; dyslexia
    in brain words, 104

brain words established through, 5
building in second through sixth grade, 107–122
connection between reading and, 28–29
curriculum selection for, 115–117
developmental phases in, 64, 67–68
developmental sequence in, 63
developmental theory and, 21–22
as differentiator between good and poor readers, 65
early assessment of, 74–81
in early literacy, 20
errors in, 104
in everyday writing, 82–84
Gentry phases of development, 23–24, 69–70
as goal in reading instruction, 48
importance of, 3
importance of teaching, 30–32
inadequacy of instruction in, 56–59
instruction in, 115–122
invented, 4, 65–67
literacy instruction and, 2
meaning and, 27, 104
memorization of, 94–95
phase observation of, 10, 63–85
power of, 88
practice in and meaning, 114–115
practice in and reading improvement, 29
practice sessions, 121
pretests, 110, 115–116
self-teaching hypothesis, 25–26
in spell-to-read, 115–122
spell-to-read and, 29–32
syllable types and, 118–119
teacher feedback on, 97–100
teaching the right words at the right time in, 58
technology and, 60
whole language instruction on, 50
word permanency and, 117–122
word reading and, 69–73
word selection for, 100–101, 111, 112
spelling books, 116–117
spell-to-read approach, 4–5
    assessment in, 102
    benefits of, 29–32